Pangyrus

Eight

NTRODUCING

Sickness and In Health:
fe in the Pandemic and Beyond

Pangyrus

For information about permission to reproduce selections from this book,
please write to Permissions at info@pangyrus.com
The text of this book is set in Palatino
with display text set in Crimson and Baskerville

Composition by Abraar Chaudhry
Cover design by Doug Woodhouse

Editor: Greg Harris
Managing Editor: Cynthia Bargar
Online Editor: Amanda Lewis
Fiction Editor: Anne Bernays
Associate Fiction Editor: Indu S. Guzman
Poetry Editor: Cheryl Clark Vermeulen
Nonfiction Editor: Artress Bethany White
Associate Nonfiction Editor: Susan Wyssen
Zest! Editor: Deborah Norkin
Comics Editor: Dan Mazur
Schooled Editors: Christelle Siantis & Michaela Gaziano
Health Editor: Erica Reaves
Communications Manager: Susannah Lutz
Graphic & Web Designer: Esther Weeks
Editorial Assistant: Tessa Rudolph
Readers and Copy Editors: Emery Behanna, Erica Bronstein, Susannah
Borysthen-Tkacz, Ceillie Clark-Keane, Shalene Gupta, Chris Hartman, Molly
Howes, Judy Kessler, Lisa Lee, Jess McCann, Deborah Mead, Elizabeth Ogle,
Dharani Persaud, Anna Reidister, Katiana Rodriguez, Michael Schermerhorn

Logo Design: Ted Ollier
Pangyrus
c/o Greg Harris, 79 JFK St, B202
Cambridge, MA 02138
pangyrus.com

Contents

Special Table of Contents

In Sickness and In Health: Life in the Pandemic and Beyond

Pangyrus

Note from the Editor

*A*s I sit down to write this editor's note, it's with a feeling that something ails us, as a body politic. Specifically, suspense is killing us.

The election ends—except for the insurrection. The vaccines finally roll out—but COVID-19 mutates faster. We don't know, as Joe Biden and Kamala Harris come off their heavily fortified inauguration, whether the country now starts to heal—or falls deeper into warring camps.

Suspense keeps us turning pages in a book. It makes the doomscroll of news irresistible. It's a state of arousal, of heightened emotion, of sharpened cognition, of being primed to see clues and relationships and underlying truths in the unfolding of events.

Until we burn out.

When we can't turn it off, it's anxiety, insomnia, hyperfocus that's also, weirdly, the inability to focus, physical breakdown, and ultimately, in worst cases, the learned helplessness that nothing I do matters or the defensive aggression of paranoia—the rush of nonsensical connections that, to a fevered brain, *finally makes sense of it all.*

Or so I hear. Asking for a friend.

People have speculated all kinds of reasons for our love of reading literature. I'd propose one less remarked on: reading is astonishingly like being held. We immerse ourselves, through the experience of language, in the unified, considered expression of someone else's consciousness. Someone else's wisdom and art, in telling stories, in weaving language, brings new patterns to our perceptions. Teaches us to see, and feel, more deeply.

All the more so if we've snuggled into an overstuffed chair, or curled up with blankets, in a peaceful room where the pages are the only illuminated corner.

"I can't read books anymore," too many friends have told me recently. The demands of the outside world, about which they felt they could do little, commanded so much urgency.

Yet here is what is waiting between covers: peace. Focus. Insight. Connection. Perspective. A pace set by imagination and consideration, not twitchy click-finger algorithms. It's when we feel we *can't* read that we must.

The good news is, once we start, the habit builds. A space gets cleared for consciousness, for integrity, for thought.

We bring you this, our 8th volume in print, with a host of special features. It's free of pop-ups, alerts, pings, messages, apps, webpages, and links other than the ones you form yourselves. You hold in your hands a great tool for being in touch with the rhythms of breath, the unfolding of idea. Use it. Flip to something. Feel the air as you do, the feathery page-ends on your thumb. Search, with your eye, for delight. Absorption.

Which is not to say that *Pangyrus 8* lacks urgency. This is a magazine of engagement, of connection, of discovery—and what we discovered in 2020, when these poems and stories came to us,

was that, far too often, we'd be called on to wrestle with the limit of what's bearable.

Early in the pandemic we launched a new section, "In Sickness and In Health," to respond to the overwhelming new facts governing our lives. The response was heartening, and led to pieces that we read not just as editors, but as people grateful to the writers for putting into words aspects of experience we, too, struggled with. From Xiaoly Li's "Your Fire and Thunder," a tragic, posthumous tribute to a voice of warning, to pieces like L.M. Brown's "What We Worried About," that registered the seismic shift in our priorities, we learned, we grew, we recognized.

All the more so as the Black Lives Matter movement sprang into anguished protest. Writers wrestled with the difficulties through their lives and their art , and the results are some of the most powerful pieces we've ever published, "For Greenwood" by Celeste Cosme and "Love Letter to My Soon To Be Thirteen-Year-Old Son" by Ryane Nicole Granados.

These pieces and more are woven throughout *Pangyrus Eight's* mix of stories, poems, and comics, all of it designed to spirit you away and bring you back more here than you've ever been before. Read Martín Espada's "The Spotlight at the Corner...", Pamela Painter's "The Red Bicycle" and "Simple Math," Charles Bernstein's ringing verse ('we were the fire before the fire was ours'), Belle (Bom) Kim's instantly relatable "Covid Diaries."

Read—and enjoy.

Greg Harris
Cambridge, Massachusetts

Your Fire and Thunder

by Xiaoly Li

—for Dr. Li Wenliang

They muzzled
your warning —

the virus spread.

It killed you, killed
the family of generations,
and killed those delaying weddings,

those collapsed on the street
before time could serve them,

and those crushed by
unrelenting work to save.

Torn cries of the
Lunar New Year

muffled by marching songs
evaporating to floating
clouds that will

come back as rain.

Author's Comment: *The day Dr. Li Wenliang died of coronavirus, I could not hold in my tears. He died of the very virus he had sounded an alarm over before it was officially announced. He was disciplined for his warning and had to confess to the so-called mistake. The price for ignorance and political self-service is high. The whole world is paying for it. Let us emerge humbler, wiser and stronger out of this pandemic of the century.*

TEARS

by Vi Khi Nao

for Bree Cameron

In the *Year* and *Era* of Our *Quarantine*
Your tears wander the vacant streets at night,
One *fluvial* wet *footstep* at a time
Desolate & forgiving & not uniformed
Before arriving to the atrium of my *breath*

Though aware of each other's existence
I know your tears & mine never met
Never walk the same forgotten bridge, the same boulevard,
the same graveyard, the same church, the same coffee shop,
the same restaurant, the same bar, the same telephone booth,
    the same tree
Until all souls, old and young, and their cluttered, cancellable
    contents are forced indoors

But, now, just yesterday your tears fall from their bewildering height
Onto my digital sleeves in broad daylight
Soaking the cities of my enemy, flooding the crumpled bodies of
    old electronic
newspapers, sedating an army of words &
    images as they float downstream
in the digital stream towards their untimely deaths
As you introduced yourself to me for the very first time

If your tears & my tears could hold each other's hands
While wandering quietly & soundlessly through the different
        Instagram *corridors* as
we intimately   share the history of our melancholy,
        our demoralizing
lives before the Great Flood, the *1918 Flu Pandemic,* before the era
of the *Me Too Movement,* before the Great Depression

If *your* tears & *my* tears could fall asleep *together*
        on this *pillow* and its
devastatingly beautiful *pillowcase* called *poetry*
Our tears could come home after many years of meaningless,
        futile travels, get on
their pluvial knees to sink and soak until they are free of their
        human debris
Wouldn't that be so awesome, Bree?

Onion Skin

by Judy Sandler

Day 6, coronavirus quarantine, 6 pm:

You stand over the kitchen sink, a large onion in your left hand, a Global Sai kitchen knife in your right hand. This is a familiar position in the best of times, and it has become even more common for you since the coronavirus forced the world inside; you turn to cooking for the production, comfort, and satisfaction of it. You stare at the onion and you can't help but think that lately, you feel a lot like this onion in your left hand.

You peel the brown, papery layer of skin from the onion. It falls away easily into the bottom of the stainless-steel sink. It's identical to your outer layer. It appears protective and dependable. But look how easily it peels off. You feel like that part of you has been stripped, that you stand more exposed than ever. The outer layer is so easy to hold onto in good times, socializing with friends, working out in gyms, eating in restaurants late into the evening. You grasp onto your outer skin. But quarantined with your family, this layer drops off like the loose, brown skin of the onion. You barely have to pull at it, you can peel it with your hands.

You touch the next layer of the onion. It is slightly wet, having been protected by the tougher covering for so long. This skin is pale yellow, delicate, inexperienced at being exposed. You stare at the onion and think about last night, that part of you that became exposed, that part protected in times when the rules are clear and you always know what to do. Last night you didn't know if your son's friend, Liam, could come over and download a game from your son's computer. You didn't know if he could come in the house, or if it was safer if he just stayed on the porch. You didn't know if he should stay in his car in the driveway. You didn't even know if he should be touching your son's computer at all in this time of social distancing, when the virus lives on keyboards and phones. The answer should have been no. No, Liam can't come over, no he can't touch your computer, no your friend can't be that close.

The layer is exposed: you can't say no. You walk away from conflict, even in regular times. Liam arrives because you can't say no. He stays in the car in the driveway because you come up with a lame compromise about how he can download the game, but not come into the house. Your husband isn't afraid to say no, and shouts at your son, "This is how the virus spreads! One friend comes over. Get Liam out of the driveway!" Voices are raised. Harsh words are exchanged.

"You all are crazy!" Your son shouts as he heads out the door to greet Liam.

"I'm tired of being the bad guy!" Your husband pleads with you, as he storms to his studio. "You are going to infect us all. You have to tell him no, he cannot have his friends randomly arriving at the house."

This layer feels raw, unexpectedly revealed anew. You examine it, like the onion in your hand. There it is, your inability to say no, your conflict averse layer. It has always been there, a problem for sure, but now it is glowing, revealed like a rabbit under a magician's hat.

You stare at the onion in your hand and keep peeling. Now the onion is weeping, tiny pearls of iridescent liquid emerging. It is more sensitive to the touch than the layer before it, and it appears in your hand as white, transparent, and slippery to the touch. Another layer revealed, in the rapidly changing, quickly thinning and collapsing walls of the socially distant life you live now. You stare at this layer of the onion. It is the layer of selfishness in you, the one that bends rules because the rules aren't convenient. The layer that in normal times is rarely exposed or questioned. But in these days of threat of illness and quarantine, the stakes are higher and the consequences grim. This last conversation you had with your husband and son plays in your head like an annoying song.

"I'm going to play lacrosse on the field at Gilman," your son says, referring to his old school.

"Sounds good," you tell him.

"Who will be there? How many people are coming to the field? Do you understand that every time you come in contact with a new person, you expose yourself, your parents, and your grandmother in a new way?" Your husband reins in the rules again.

"Oh my God, Dad, we are on an open field. I won't touch anyone. I won't come within six feet of anyone. I understand what you are saying." He grabs his lacrosse equipment and hauls it outside, pulling the door shut behind him.

Your husband looks at you. "Can you help here? Do you understand the consequences of him being with a bunch of boys on a field?"

You stare at him, tight-lipped and teary. This layer is exposed. You think you can help enforce the rules, but it does not come naturally to you. You are not a good follower of rules. You stand in front of him; this layer appears naked and selfish.

The onion is still in your left hand, the knife in your right. You are down to the core now. It is a small ball, white and exposed. The core is slippery, and the skin has veins, like the very thin blue arteries that run up the inside of your arm. You observe every line, each place the skin might tear apart from the center. Deep inside the onion a small green sprout emerges. Oh, you think, maybe this onion has been in the refrigerator too long. Then you reconsider. The green is new growth from the inside. No one can see it, concealed, growing and gaining strength from the layers of protection. It may never get there, forced back inside by the stronger outer layers, but you notice that the bud is there. It can change and grow. This global pandemic shines a spotlight through to your core. When you emerge from this quarantine, from this house, from this stance in front of the kitchen sink, knife in one hand, onion in the other, you will remember: the green sprout is buried deep inside, but alive.

The Paint

by James Stewart III

Sitting on a basketball at half-court, Jim is telling the boys the fundamentals of the game. Mason and Jimmy listen intently. Well, as intently as can be expected from a five and seven-year-old. Everything is just so interesting on a warm, sunny day in the suburbs: a kid sliding down the nearby playground equipment, workers repaving a residential driveway across the street, birds doing bird things. They're alone except for those birds pecking at something near the border between asphalt and grass that surrounds the court.

It's a day off on the weekend, which in retail is sacrosanct. A high-holy day all in itself. Usually, when Jim has a day off he works a side-job, today he's got nothing going on. Part of him feels guilty, though. Always.

"That area there, right around the basket," he says pointing at the 15 x 12 ft. rectangle, outlined by fading white lines. "That's where the game is won and lost. The paint. That's your house and you protect it at all costs."

On the South Side, Jim started playing down-low because of his size but stuck there because of his heart. In the paint the grace of the game, at times an intricately choreographed dance, devolves into gritty survivalism. Elbows fly, knees drive into thighs, one of those fast, graceful skinny motherfuckers comes in weak thinking he can get an easy layup. As they ascend towards the rim with visions of two points, perhaps a gentle finger-roll, to just flip the ball into the rim, Jim knows this man's fantasy needs some reconfiguring.

"In the paint, nobody gets anything easy."

He pushes his glasses further up the ridge of his nose, rubs his bushy, black mustache, then adjusts his high grey tube socks, two red stripes running around the top. His shorts are short. Really short.

"Can we shoot now?" Mason asks impatiently.

He decided against a shirt today since it's so hot, plus he can show off his muscles, which don't exist to anyone but himself. He flexes bones. Skin, the color of cocoa butter, blue eyes, a poorly done flattop cut by his mother, Mason's always running low on patience.

"That's all you ever wanna do," Jimmy says.

"Boys, listen and learn something."

Mason grunts. A ball hog. All attitude with an inability to hide whatever he's feeling.

"Stand up and I'll show you two how it's done."

The boys spring up, while it takes Jim longer to unfold his large frame. Standing upright he towers over his young sons descending in height by age and hues of brown, covering the spectrum so fully that only one of them is even called brown.

Jim is dark-skinned, the prevailing idea of Black in America. Jimmy is swinging his arms through the air in some approximation of the stretches he's seen basketball players do on TV. Copper-complexioned he'll be asked the rest of his life where he's from and hear guesses anywhere from Central and South America, North Africa,

South Asia, and the Middle East. He'll let them down every time he says he's from Chicago. Mason is high yellow. All brown. All black.

As soon as Jim stands, Mason grabs the ball from the ground, throws it ahead of him, chases it down, takes two dribbles, comes to a complete stop in front of the basket, pulls the ball back like a shot-putter, sends it over the front of the rim to the white polymer backboard where it thuds before rattling through the chain link net. Turning back towards Jim he shakes his head and flexes his bones in celebration. Jimmy gets the rebound.

On these courts, the sweet snapping swish of the ball through a nylon net is replaced by jangling reminiscent of loose change that the chain link provides. Much more durable for the bipolar weather of the Midwest, but also more dangerous for fingers.

Awaiting further instructions, with the childhood inability to stand still while holding a ball, Jimmy attempts to spin it on his finger. Looks so easy. He quickly finds out it's not. Spin, smack, drop, bounce. Spin, smack, drop, bounce. He settles for trying to balance it on a finger, no spin. He just ends up running in tiny circles trying to keep the ball from the asphalt as it wobbles every which way.

"Lemme try," Mason demands.

Catching the ball from Jimmy, he gives it a shot and fails. Tries again… fails. His face scrunches up, the ever-present dimples in his squirrel-cheeks compete with the wrinkles at the bridge of his nose to show his frustration. He smacks the ball with one hand, switches and smacks it with another, as if there's some answer to this mystery inside the sphere.

"Betchu guys can't do this," he announces to his family.

Mason wipes the ball on his bare stomach, tilts his head back, alllll the way back. Then holding the ball above his head with both hands, gently sets it into the groove between nose and forehead, then let's go. His neck and shoulders wiggle, hands up and ready to catch the ball if it falls.

Jim and Jimmy lock-eyes, both laughing.

"Your brother's got no sense."

Mason keeps the ball balanced for all of five, six seconds. When it falls he celebrates with the same enthusiasm he showed after making a basket.

"Now pass the ball here," Jim tells Mason. The ball's disproportionately large in the boy's hands. A thought that never occurs when grown men shoot around. Effortless moves, a chest-pass, a lay-up, a free-throw, all seem to require every ounce of strength his boys have.

Mason reaches back and lets go, the ball makes it to Jim in a bounce and a half.

"Now pay attention, we're gonna start down low, where the game's really played."

"Let's shoot three's!" blurts Mason.

"That's not what dad said. The game's in the paint," replies Jimmy, a constant check on his brother's impulses.

"Exactly, boy. All the best teams always have a big man controlling the paint. Wilt, Bill, Kareem, Moses, and Chocolate Thunder! All you kids out here tryna 'Be Like Mike,' now."

In Chicago, the history of the game reaches beyond professional contracts into the high schools and the playground. From Jim's alma mater, Hales Franciscan, people expected Sam Puckett, a smooth All-American point-guard to do great things in college and the NBA. Neither happened.

Dribbling to the block, Jim shoots a standard layup, right hand rising, balancing the ball on his palm, jumping off his left foot, right knee rising in unison with his arm as if an invisible string connects knee and elbow. The ball banks off the backboard and in.

He tries to think of the last time he played a pickup game. College, maybe? A few years after? Whatever the moment, it certainly didn't have the gravity then that he's feeling it should have now.

"See. That's the easiest shot in the game. It's simple. You want to get as close as possible, as often as possible. That's why on defense you have to keep them out of the paint. You give these shots up and they'll take advantage of you all game. If someone thinks they can get something easy from you once, they'll keep coming in and testing you until you stop them."

"I can do that. I'll make those all day!" says Mason.

"No, he can't! Let me try first," Jimmy replies.

Jim passes Jimmy the ball. The boy dribbles it toward the right-hand side of the rim and takes a shot. Jimmy jumps off his right foot, instead of his left, the ball hits off the bottom of the rim and comes off it with a loud clank. The ball ricochets and hits Jimmy on the top of his head with a hollow plonk.

Jim smiles and Mason laughs, while Jimmy, embarrassed, runs after the ball which shot off the court onto the surrounding grass.

"That was alright, but you jumped off the wrong foot. You'll get it next time. Let your brother try."

Jimmy, still on the grass, reaches back and throws the ball to Mason football-style.

"I'll do it right."

For Mason, smaller and weaker than his older brother, basketball 101 is still a physical impossibility. In order just to get the ball above the rim it's essential for him to get in a deep squat, cock the ball back to his ear, and catapult it. The ball bounces off the backboard and in. Before it jangles through the net, he's already grunting and flexing bone.

"SEE THAT!"

Jim rolls his eyes.

"You made it, but practice isn't always about making shots. It's about learning how to play the game right." Jim means to deflate Mason's ego, just a bit.

"Yeah," Jimmy agrees.

The boys go through a few more rounds of layups, the ball gaining a gritty, dusty feeling. It ricochets off the rim into the grass, through wood chips in the playground, and into the street a few times, Jim shouting as the boys begin to run into it absentmindedly. His deep, loud, voice stops time, the boys freeze immediately, then look both ways. Of course, no cars are coming by on this boring street.

They run up a small grass incline back towards the court. Jimmy has the ball on his hip, and it's just as wide as his waist.

"Here. Pass it again," Jim says, thinking about the next lesson. Raising it above his head Jimmy hurls the ball towards his dad.

Jim has to keep the boys shooting to keep them interested, but they can shoot layups left handed without mastering their right, plus they're not strong enough to shoot anything other than layups. The key to the game isn't offense anyway.

He knows the game is really all about defense. Defense and rebounding. Anybody could do these things, but the key is they have to want to. It can't be faked. Thankless toil, the drudgery that builds winners, that builds champions, an attitude, unrelenting persistence. Brings you nothing but bruises, welts, and floor burns. Your body, you give to the team, a sacrifice. You can't let them down.

Love Letter to My Soon to Be 13-Year-Old Black Son
by Ryane Nicole Granados

Dear Sonshine,

That's what I call you because the mere sight of your go big or go home smile is like the sun filtering through our shutters on a bright California day. It's the summer before your 13th birthday but for months now you've been reiterating that you're taller than me, that you can almost fit in your father's shoes, that your dreams are ever-changing: soccer player, drummer, paramedic. You are just as strong-willed as you were as a toddler, but to my delight your personality has also emerged as outgoing and kind. You are compassionate to strangers, concerned about world issues, and you are constantly, unabashedly questioning.

It is usually in these moments of inquiry where my enchantment with you turns to frustration and fear. You see son, I have lived in this Black skin longer than you have. I have learned to walk a fine line between approachable and articulate, between joy and rage. I know that the difference between coming home alive or becoming a hashtag might be the stifling of my understandable need to question someone's unjust begrudging of my humanity. So your father and I usually exchange a glance and maybe a sigh and in the small window before you disappear into your video games with friends, we try to explain to you the terrifying duality of being Black and being perceived as an adult in America.

I have never been in a rush for you to grow up. I miss the days when your cheeks ballooned like they were filled with cotton candy and your tiny hands still had that soft pudge of baby fat and unspecified preschool stickiness. I cringed in your early elementary years when well-meaning people would comment on how tall you were for your age or enthusiastic barbers would call you "little man" as you walked self-possessed into the barbershop. I wanted to stop time when you hit the double digits because as long as you were animated and adorable by society's standards you were protected, or so I thought, from the perils of racism and police brutality.

But then you turned 11. Seemingly overnight you had a huge growth spurt met with painful spasms in your legs. Your father would spend the evenings massaging your muscles and your physical pain mirrored my maternal worry that growing up could actually hurt you. This reality was magnified one afternoon when I was waiting for you outside of school. We've always taught you to never run when crossing the street. You know to only begin walking when the little man is blinking and most importantly you know Dad, Nana, or I will always be waiting on the other side to greet you.

On this particular day a police officer pulled into the crosswalk and swerved his squad car beside you yelling on his loudspeaker for you to hurry up and get across. The little white man was still blinking. At the realization that the officer's car was coming right in your direction, you froze in fear like your legs were stuck in a spasm. I could see from a distance the furrow in your brow right above the scar from when you fell and hit your head on the coffee table at two. That furrow is your questioning wrinkle: should you run, should you walk, should you put your hands up, what should you do? At that point the police officer flashed his lights at you.

At 11 years old you were admittedly the height of a 13-year-old, but you were still a child. You were still my child. I hopped out of my running car leaving your little brother strapped in his car seat and ran into the crosswalk screaming, "He is only 11 years old." Other parents, white parents, having known you since kindergarten, started screaming at the officer too. I secretly hoped their whiteness would be a shield for you. I wondered if we should yell out a catalogue of your supposed worthiness for you to be treated with human decency: that you have straight A's, play drums in a kids' rock band, that you're training in taekwondo when not participating in youth church. I lunged in front of the police car to protect you the same way I promised during the emergency C-section of your delivery that I would die for you. As the other parents were demanding the officer's badge number, he screeched his car around us all speeding through our once safeguarded school zone. Before that day, you professed you wanted to be a police officer when you grew up. You now express you want to be a paramedic because you want to help people.

In a few short months you will be the actual age that you appeared to be when you were 11. You no longer talk about that incident outside of the school and you've already begun to develop a hardened jawline where those candy-coated cheeks used to be. But one trait that remains is your questioning. *So I can't wear my black hoodie because of what happened to Trayvon? I can't go jogging anymore because of what they did to Ahmaud?* Every year of your young life, names have been added to a running list of Black bodies. They are real-life characters in a cautionary tale. We speak of them like family. They are play cousins or distant uncles who we mourn and grieve and before the sorrow extinguishes, there's another name added to the list.

When I was in middle school, around the same age as you are now, the image of Rodney King being struck repeatedly by police played on loop on the TV and still today in my tarnished dreams. I was naïve enough then to think that video proof was the same as irrefutable truth, but the older men at the corner store knew better. I would overhear them saying, "They're gonna get off" and I thought to myself such foolish old men. They knew nothing about hope and technology and the power of the tape. With the certainty that only a preteen could possess, I dismissed their comments, drowning them out with music from my Sony Walkman.

And now I'm the foolish one and you're in middle school and your fingertips scroll through countless images of hope lost and technology unheeded, your cell phone housing tragedy on tape. I repossess it trying to censor you from its content. This isn't a Hollywood movie or a video game. This is a real-life public lynching where a knee is dug into George Floyd's neck for 8 minutes and 46 seconds, causing his soul to seep out of his body as he calls out for his dead mother. I beg you to never watch it. I implore you to take a walk with me instead. We make our way to the hiking trails at the top of our street and below I can see the remnants of dilapidated buildings never rebuilt from the fires that blazed in Rodney King's name. It's a dizzying form of déjà vu. Then you tell me you want to protest.

For a moment I forget that we aren't just dealing with the pandemic of racism. There is a disease, a novel coronavirus that is killing people indiscriminately. You also have a medical procedure coming up. It's my job to keep you safe. Yet once again I feel the expressiveness I always wanted to encourage in my children becoming suppressed under the weight of a world that demands you be silent. I tell you it isn't safe for you to protest. You can't be around that many people so close to your surgery. I can see your frown tighten under your mask as your brow gives off its familiar furrow. You don't say anything to me as we walk home. In a sulk, you pop in your AirPods.

As we juggle two pandemics at once, I get to see you finding your own voice amid a new generation of burgeoning activists. I still don't let you join a protest march and for that I feel like a fraud disappointing her comrades of 1992. Instead, you decide to make your final project for your art class a tribute piece to Black lives. You marry your love of drumming and photography by taking the first drum you ever owned and repurposing it with pictures of unarmed Black men, women, and children killed because of unbridled hate. You complain that there are so many faces you can't fit them all on your drum. You mention that "a drum is like a heartbeat, so every time you play you will be playing for those whose hearts no longer beat." This is what it means to turn 13 while being Black in America.

Your drum looks like an oversized birthday cake and I can't help but feel the heartache of Tamir and Michael and Breonna's mothers who no longer get to see their children add candles to their cakes. I should be celebrating you getting older instead of begrudging it. You deserve to grow and evolve; to be happy with your friends and snarky with your parents, to make all the typical coming-of-age mistakes that any teenager might make without the added burden of your skin being weaponized against you. You are right to question why I am having the same conversations with you that Nana had with me, that your Great Granny had with Nana.

A year after you were born, the United States elected its first ever African-American president. For the bulk of your formative years, this was the only president you ever knew. Your Dad and I still chuckle at how you commented during the election season of your 9th birthday that you didn't know so many white people were running for president too.

You had a lifetime to learn that you were born under a rare banner of historical significance. Your innocence felt sacred and magical; something too sweet to correct too soon. But you are wising up now as fast as you are rising up, and I see hope in you. I see your smile like welcomed sunshine burning off the haze of June gloom. I feel you resting your long arm on my shoulder, towering over me, casting shadows in the breeze. I imagine our chorus of laughter as we sing Happy Birthday loud and off-key. Stevie Wonder's version of course. I see your destiny. And in these last few months before you turn the long-awaited 13, I see that watching you age has been the ultimate gift to me. In return, I offer you these words of love simply stated to my soon-to-be teenage Black son,

"Now and forevermore, in a world that needs your light, you matter!"

Love, Mom

*How to Make a No-Sew Coronavirus Mask From a Poem**
by Wendy Drexler

1. After you've read this poem, place it
    on your kitchen table
2. From the top of the poem, fold down a flap of your fear;
    from the bottom, a flap of hope.
3. Turn this poem over and smooth it tenderly
    with the side of your hand. You will
    no longer be able to read
    this poem. Trust it.
4. Feed an elastic hairband over each end of this poem
    the way you once gathered the strands
    of your daughter's ponytail.
5. Now fold in both ends of the poem
    until they overlap like waves
    on the bay.
6. Turn over the poem and plump
    the pleats.
7. Secure the elastic hairbands of this poem
    around the shells of your ears.
8. Wear this poem as if your life
    depended on it.

*
Note to User:
This poem is not guaranteed to save you or the world.
However, evidence suggests that a poem may help you
get through one more day.

Seeing Red

by Pamela Painter

How long has that bicycle been out there he asks his wife. She's still seated at the breakfast table, slapping around the morning paper. He's peering through the bay window at the ten-speed bike chained to a skinny pole beneath a sign about Cambridge's parking restrictions. Surely he has passed it on his daily walk to campus.

His wife joins him at the window, says I wonder who abandoned it?

He thinks why *abandoned*? "I'm going to take a closer look." When his wife, still in her ratty bathrobe, follows him outside, he is annoyed.

It's a man's bike, not yet rusted, with two side pouches and a bell. Odd that no one in the neighborhood mentioned it. Neither the economist next door nor the widow archivist across the street. Dog shit is melting nearby. His wife flicks dust from the grey fenders with the hem of her robe, squeezes the rusted bell.

He jumps.

"Sounds like a wild turkey's screech," she says. "The Animal Rescue League should know about this turkey?" She rings the bell a second time, a third.

"Stop that." He likes wild turkeys. He admires their heavy bodies, so ponderous and slow, yet deliberate when finally taking flight. "Let's see how long it stays here," he says.

He is tempted to pat the bike when he passes it on the way to his Poetry Seminar. He doesn't tell his students, anyone, about the bike. He saves it for himself.

Walking home from class the next week, he immediately sees the change. The bicycle is red. Tires, pouches, bell, the creased seat and thin spokes—all glow a lurid red he knows he's seen before. Sure enough, in the foyer, a can of red paint has dripped onto an old copy of *New York Review of Books*.

"Did you see it?" his wife asks, moving to the window. "Did you??

Why, he thinks. "Why?" he says.

"Now it's almost art," she says. "You can write a poem about it."

It is not art. And it is not a poem. Will he ever write another poem?

Three days later she calls him at school and starts right in, "You'll never guess...." But somehow he knows: the bicycle is gone.

"If you hadn't painted it, the bicycle would still be there," he tells his wife with strange certainty.

His wife says, "You'll write a better poem this way."

At home, he bends down beside the skinny pole, stirs two patches of red-flecked dirt where the bike's wheels touched earth. The severed ends of the chain are bright silver. He carries the chain inside and coils it into an old hat he'll take with him when he leaves. Who would believe it was the last straw.

The Stoplight at the Corner Where Somebody Had to Die
by Martín Espada

They won't put a stoplight on that corner till somebody dies, my father
would say. *Somebody has to die.* And my mother would always repeat:
Somebody has to die. One morning, I saw a boy from school facedown
in the street, there on the corner where somebody had to die. I saw
the blood streaming from his head, turning the black asphalt blacker.
He heard the bells from the ice cream truck and ran across the street,
somebody in the crowd said. *The guy in the car never saw him.*
And somebody in the crowd said: *Yeah. The guy never saw him.*

Later, I saw the boy in my gym class, standing in the corner of the gym.
Maybe he was a ghost, haunting the gym as I would sometimes haunt
the gym, standing in the corner, or maybe he wasn't dead at all. They
never put the stoplight there, at the corner where somebody had to die,
where the guy in the car never saw him, where the boy heard the bells.

Love Letters 1918

by Olive Malcolm

Dearest Olive:

Once more I am going to the country club with Ernest Vogt, but there are about two minutes before he comes for me. We paraded through Louisville this afternoon (my battalion & me) along with a mounted battalion of the F.A.R.D.. . . . as part of a parade to boost Liberty Bonds. It was my first parade, and I was quite enraptured with it. The "Boy Scouts" (which is the name my platoon has been given by the rest of the battery) led the way, and it was quite gratifying to hear such remarks from the curb as "Best line I've seen yet." or "They're a clean looking bunch of little fellows."*

I have to be back at camp at 8:30 tomorrow morn for a fool medical exam which I took at Fort Jackson, but which I have to take over again — such is the way of the army (our papers were lost I think.)

Now I must away. I wish I were going to see you instead of going to the country club. But I am looking forward to seeing you at Thanksgiving. I wonder if it will be here or there....

*Field Artillery Replacement Depot

Good-bye, my very Dearest,
Gil

This letter, dated September 28, 1918, is one of a collection of 171 letters Gilbert Robertson Glorieux and Olive Mortimer Remington exchanged over a period that encompassed a world war and the last truly global pandemic. The letters moved from my parents' basement in Urbana to mine in Cambridge in 1984, when my parents died. In 2017, I was going to throw them away, unread. I was intrigued, though, by the three-cent stamps and addresses that suggested a time when just a name and a town was sufficient to find someone (like "Gilbert R. Glorieux, Springfield, New Jersey" and "Olive Remington c/o Robt. Gemmell, Salt Lake City, Utah"). More than that: Olive Mortimer Remington was my mother. Why had she kept these letters so many years? Who was this Gil?

My curiosity aroused, I removed the letters from their envelopes, arranged them chronologically, and started to piece together the story of a love affair that my mother, while alive, had never hinted at.

It began two years before the letter above, in Freehold, New York in 1916, where Gil met Olive at a sledding party. She was a freshman at Vassar and he a junior at Princeton. For a year, the letters show Gil struggling with Virgil and Cicero, and Olive concentrating on writing and directing the Sophomore Show.

Then, in the spring of 1917, war made its appearance. Gil, distressed by Woodrow Wilson's failure to come to the aid of France and England, joined a group of Princeton men who went to France to serve in the American Field Ambulance Corp attached to the French Army. In letters from France he writes of wild carriage drives through Bois de Boulogne, the delicious petits gateaux in a little village — and the war:

The ruined town below us… looked for all the world as though it was painted on canvas, and the flashing of the shells, was like some imaginative stage manager's production, while the queer light of the dawning day made you all the more sure it was not real.

But it was real, and men were dying there in horrible strangling death, with these infernal shells landing all around them. They deserved it I suppose, for they started all this sort of thing, and it is simply their own work being turned against them, but for all that I felt very sorry for them. I wish our army would not use any gas.

Olive's letters give a glimpse of the home front. She wrote about college life, collecting money wearing a Red Cross uniform on the trains between New Jersey and New York City, and her summer as a counselor at a Welfare Camp in Peekskill, teaching swimming and leading New York factory shop girls up mountain trails.

In November of 1917, Gilbert returned from France determined to contribute more to the war effort by joining the U.S. Army Aviation Service. He was also intent on seeing Olive and in anticipation of Olive's Christmas vacation he wrote from his parents' home in Springfield, N.J., December 17:

When I came home, Olive darling, I felt that the trip would be a thousand times repaid if I could see you for a day or two. And now I'm going to see a lot of you for three weeks, and see you occasionally for a long while after that. The Fates are good to us, Olive, —good to me at any rate. And before you go back to college perhaps—but we must wait and see. Olive, my love, it would be impossible for me to fall in love with someone else—I would feel as though I were tied to a post; perhaps a fine straight marble post, but it would be the same nevertheless. No one else in the world could ever make me feel that she understood as you do. No matter what you decide, Olive, and no matter where I shall be in after life, you shall always be the girl I love.

Gil

There is no account of that Christmas vacation, but surely it lived up to Gil's anticipation as they became secretly engaged. Olive wanted the whole world to know but Gil knew his parents would not approve. He was twenty-two and had yet to receive his bachelor's degree or prepare for a profession.

They didn't have much time together during the coming months, for in late January Gil was confined to bed rest with a weak and enlarged heart and a bad case of jaundice— "I'm as yellow as a daffodil," he wrote. In February, Olive had an appendectomy and spent a long time in hospital recuperating and then had to catch up with schoolwork.

The war continued, as did Gil's desire to be in it. By May his heart settled down. He took the medical exam for aviation and failed it, but he managed to talk his way into the Artillery and was ordered immediately to Fort Jackson, S.C. for training. Olive spent the summer of 1918 in Salt Lake City visiting her Aunt Belle Gemmell, a physician, and her husband, an engineer in charge of the big copper mine. They wrote daily; the letters, carried by the continental railroad between boot camp and the Rocky Mountains, show a couple deeply in love. On July 21, Olive wrote from "Brighton," Aunt Belle's cabin in the mountains:

Gil belovedest,

You're here tonight—almost really—The whole canyon—it widens out to a valley here, nearly a mile across—is white with moon light. The tall skinny firs seem sky high along side our cabin—and the mountains look Oh so climbable. We'd go up the Twin Lake Trail, You & I, if you were here. It's a wide trail, cut out of the side of the mountain —sheer drop to Silver Lake (in our back yard) on the east of it—so we'd be in full moon light all the ways—From the top of the dam, at the head of the lakes, the valley is hidden—and you look straight across to Mt. Majestic—it seems near enough to pat. We'd build a fire up there to keep us warm after our climb. Then we'd come down slowly.

It makes my throat ache—just writing about it, Gil. I think we're going to love each other a very great deal as time goes along. I looked across the eastward mountains tonight—and wondered whether you were loving me...

I'd not burden you with loving—for anything in all the world. Do you see that I worry about that sometimes?

Goodnight Dearest,
Olive

Gil's reply, from Columbia, S.C. on July 29:

My Dearest Love:—

You wrote me a beautiful letter telling how in your dreams, we climbed the mountain trail in the moon-light, and then you said you would not have your love a burden to me. No, Dearest, you would not, and you could not if we lived to be a thousand years old. I love the moon light on the mountains, the wind in the trees, and the broad blue sky, but more than these, my Darling, I love you. You are to me all that there is to live for —Do you think your love can be a burden to me? Some day, Heart of Mine, Some day I will come back to you and then —it doesn't matter much where we are —we shall be happy. And there are so many things to do together and so many places to visit —but all that really matters is that we'll be together.

Good-night My Love,
Gil

That "someday" kept getting delayed by the army. After Gil finished basic training, for a short time he was an instructor in typography at Fort Jackson and then was transferred to officer's training at Camp Zachary Taylor in Louisville, KY.

It was from Camp Zachary Taylor that the letter came that I opened with, from September 28, 1918. Its date is significant. On September 24 the Louisville newspaper had reported that more than one hundred soldiers at Camp Zachary Taylor had come down with influenza. A day later the number had climbed to 262. By the end of the month 2,100 were sick. On the 27th of September the camp imposed a partial quarantine, prohibiting soldiers from entering theaters, restaurants and public places.

The quarantine did not stop either marching or country club gatherings, however, as witnessed by Gil's letter. It was only three days later, on October 1st, that Gil wrote:

Olive Dearest—

Hark to my woeful tale —I have the "Flu". I was taken sick yesterday and sent over to this emergency hospital with Hollister, a man from my battery. We were lucky enough to get bunks together, so we console each other.

I have a very light form of it —not at all serious —so you are not to worry. It's a nuisance that's all, for we have to stay in quarantine for seven days…

Olive Darling don't be alarmed if you don't hear from me for a few days. It is sort of hard to write in bed; You know I am always thinking of you anyway —and loving you with all my heart.

Good-night my Dearest.,
Gil

Never wanting to give Olive cause for worry, Gil wrote a cheerful note from the hospital, on October 3rd, 1918:

Olive Dearest —

This morning I was dozing in my bunk when a corporal arrived with a bucket of water, a cake of soap and a towel. "Hello", said I. "Going to wash the floor?"

He looked at me scornfully and said, "Wash your face!"

I protested that I had already washed my face, but he said the order was that number 22 was to wash his face.
So I washed vigorously while the corporal sat on the end of my bunk and eyed me critically. When I had finished I did it all over again, because he still looked so critical.

At last I asked him if he saw any improvement. "Not much," he said shaking his head mournfully, "but if you was to get a shave you'd do all right."

So I did shave off my long black beard this afternoon, and now I feel quite fit. I am improving at a great rate, and hope that I may be allowed to go back to my battery in a few days. If I can get back before Monday I am quite sure that I need not loose any time at the school.

The saddest thing about being in this "hospital" is that your letters are over at the battery, and they are not allowed to send them over. But what a lot of them there will be when I get back!

I have been dreaming very nice dreams of you, Olive Dear, and all the wonderful things that are going to happen some day.

Good Night Dearest,
Gil x

Many of Olive's letters did not survive but the one from Vassar of October 6th did:

Gil dear,

I'm sorry not to have written —We've had a bad time here too. Winifred Adam (she was the very tall, pretty girl —you met her in the Grand Central) grew worse on Thursday, and Friday night we knew there was no hope. She fought hard —but it was the most severe kind of pneumonia and she didn't live thru the night. It's a rather impossible thing to believe —Here she was —in her room last week —and gone entirely now. Her Mother has been wonderful —I've never seen such calm bravery. We're going down to the service in town this afternoon so I'll mail this on the way.

Jet is much better —they don't think she has pneumonia after all. The doctors here have things pretty well in hand. All our colds are well, or getting well.

I had no mail yesterday —I hope that doesn't mean you're worse, Dear. I've been very anxious—

Dearest love to you,
Olive

On October 10th, after receiving Olive's letter, Gil sent a Western Union Telegram:
LOUISVILLE, KY TO MISS OLIVE REMINGTON, VASSAR COLLEGE VERY SORRY TO HEAR OF WINFRED ADAM'S DEATH. ALSO SORRY TO HEAR THAT JET HAS BEEN ILL. HAVE BEEN MOVED TO THE BASE HOSPITAL AND

AM MORE COMFORTABLE. HAVE BRONCHITIS AND THERE IS NO DAN-
GER. HOPE TO REJOIN MY BATTERY IN FIVE OR SIX DAYS. DO NOT WORRY.
WITH LOVE GIL

On October 13th, Mortimer Remington, Olive's father, sent a West-
ern Union Telegram to Olive at Vassar College.
GILBERTS FAMILY HAVE GONE TO LOUISVILLE TO TAKE CARE OF HIM. HE
HAS PNEUMONIA FAMILY WILL KEEP ME INFORMED AND I WILL IMMEDI-
ATELY INFORM YOU. FAMILY AT SEELBACK HOTEL WILL ACT AS NURSES
YOU MUST NOT THINK OF GOING MAY REMOVE HIM TO PRIVATE HOSPI-
TAL FOR SPECIAL CARE

On October 14th, a telegram was sent to Major Remington Pier 2
Hoboken, N.J.:
GILBERT DIED SATURDAY MORNING. TELL OLIVE. JEAN GLORIEUX

Letters of sympathy and love came from Olive's mother and father,
from classmates and teachers and Henry Nobles McCracken, the
president of Vassar. The obituary for Gilbert in the newspaper "The
Sunday Call" of Newark, N.J. ended:

*Mr. Glorieux and Miss Olive Remington, daughter of Mrs. Mortim-
er Remington of 312 Belleville Avenue, this city, were engaged in mar-
riage, and it had been planned to make formal public announcement of the
engagement next month.*

I suspect Jean, Gil's older sister, was a confidante of the young
couple and was responsible for the last paragraph. A few weeks
later Jean wrote to Olive:

On Saturday I mailed a little box to you & hope you receive it all right.

It is a ring which I had made for you from one of Gilbert's cuff links. I thought you would like something you could wear and he used his links so constantly I wanted you to have one.

I wonder what happened to that ring and I ponder the sadness of Olive's last year at college. She struggled with Gil's death and sometimes tried to find solace in writing letters to him, perhaps because letters had played so great a part of their relationship she found it a way to hold on to him. The last one I found was written January 16, 1921, more than two years after his death.

Gil dear,

I'm crying—over the kind of person I am, because it isn't as you would have me. I'm ashamed of me, and the things I seek & want & do, and my failure to do anything that might make you glad, or make you love me. It's more than ashamed, it's afraid, and desolate, Because I want you—I want so to have you still love me—and I don't see how you can.

And I think my belief that you're still you—living isn't a much thought out belief—I think of you so, because I can't bear not to—And I wonder if you've grown very far ahead, away from me.

Oh my Dear, everything fine I want to be, or to do is tied up in you. it isn't just that I cling to you, the memory and thought of you, because you were my happiness—but because—It is your ideals, and love that count. I think you'd be glad— if you still care—if I could have your kind of happiness here. Oh I'm weak, weak, weak. Oh only to know you care, now, when I don't deserve it and want you so. I must stop being sobbey—and sorry for myself. I'll try and be a good sport and an always strong lover, but it wouldn't seem much use if it weren't on your account. Ohh Gil, love me if you can still.

Olive

In 1922, Olive, now 25 years old, went to Europe and in Paris met 28-year-old Marcus Selden Goldman. Marcus, like Gil, had served in the French ambulance corps. He'd stayed on to study in France and write for the New York Herald Tribune. Mama told us children that she and Papa fell in love on first meeting. I am the youngest of their four children and am glad that Olive, who loved Gil so much, found another man, my father, whom she could love as well.

At Camp Zachary Taylor, in Louisville, where Gil was stationed, 22,000 cases of the flu were reported in October 1918 and nearly 1,500 soldiers died. Estimates of deaths worldwide were over twenty million. The Great War ended, the nations were exhausted and the allies wanted only to celebrate victory. They knew not where it came from, nor how to fight it, and chose to try and forget it and hope it would never return.

Four Poems

by Charles Bernstein

Loose Lips Lift All Slips

It wasn't so long ago
and then it was. Sliding
till you hit false bottom,
wrestling metaphor for
sleep. It wasn't so long
and then it was. I'd
keep saying it but
I know you heard me,
even when you didn't.

Freudian Slap

An old man's best friend
is the past. Aggrievement's

not the end of politics

but a point of contact.
Solidarity of sleights

slips into crystal nights

as compulsory illiberalism's
hypnopompous ardour sours

in the mind's preternatural

larder. Everyday can't be
yesterday since tomorrow is

over before today is done.

You can decide what you
will do but not what you'

ll want. *Fade out*

to the sounds of Shak
Shuka and his Israel/Palestine

Arkestra, coming to you

from the Cosmogonic Ballroom
in midtown Manhattan.

The Gift Outright

You break it
you bought into
it. We were
the fire before
the fire was
ours. Now it's
theirs. There is
no hope greater

than despair &
despair is no
hope at all.

True North Is Just South of Here

North of the north pole
South of desire
I found my love
Lone and grey
Sailing for the morrow.
"How far is that?"
I asked, despaired
But she'd not tell
Not even to wind's
whispering spells.
Though flash of
Cosmos was in our
Sights, we'd little hope
Prolong the night.
Little hope but lots
Of whines, living already
On leveraged time.
Little hope and plenty
Of rime, here in a
Muddled middle
Piping signs.

Northern Machines

by Tracey Anderson

I have been drawing what I call Northern Machines since I was a child. I grew up in Edinburgh, Scotland, an avid card game player and collector, as well as a comics nut. These cards are a result of both of those passions combining togther, and of my recent exposure to Myriorama. Cut them out, shuffle them together, pick a few and make a comic based on your own inner stories. For me there is nothing quite so exciting as unwrapping new cards and finding out how they add to the overall narrative. No one story is the final story.

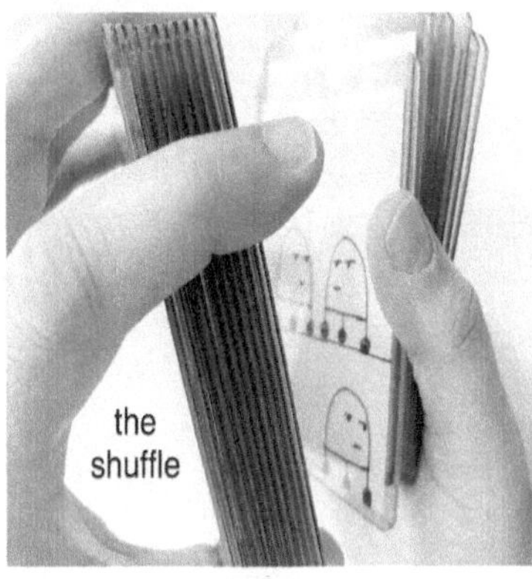

the
shuffle

Tracey Anderson is currently a public school Instructional Technology Specialist at Provincetown IB Schools on Cape Cod. She graduated from Edinburgh College of Art in Scotland, where she studied Drawing and Painting. She draws every day. Her work can be seen and supported at: **www.poorhooligans.com**

the
layout

the
comic

northern machines

northern machines

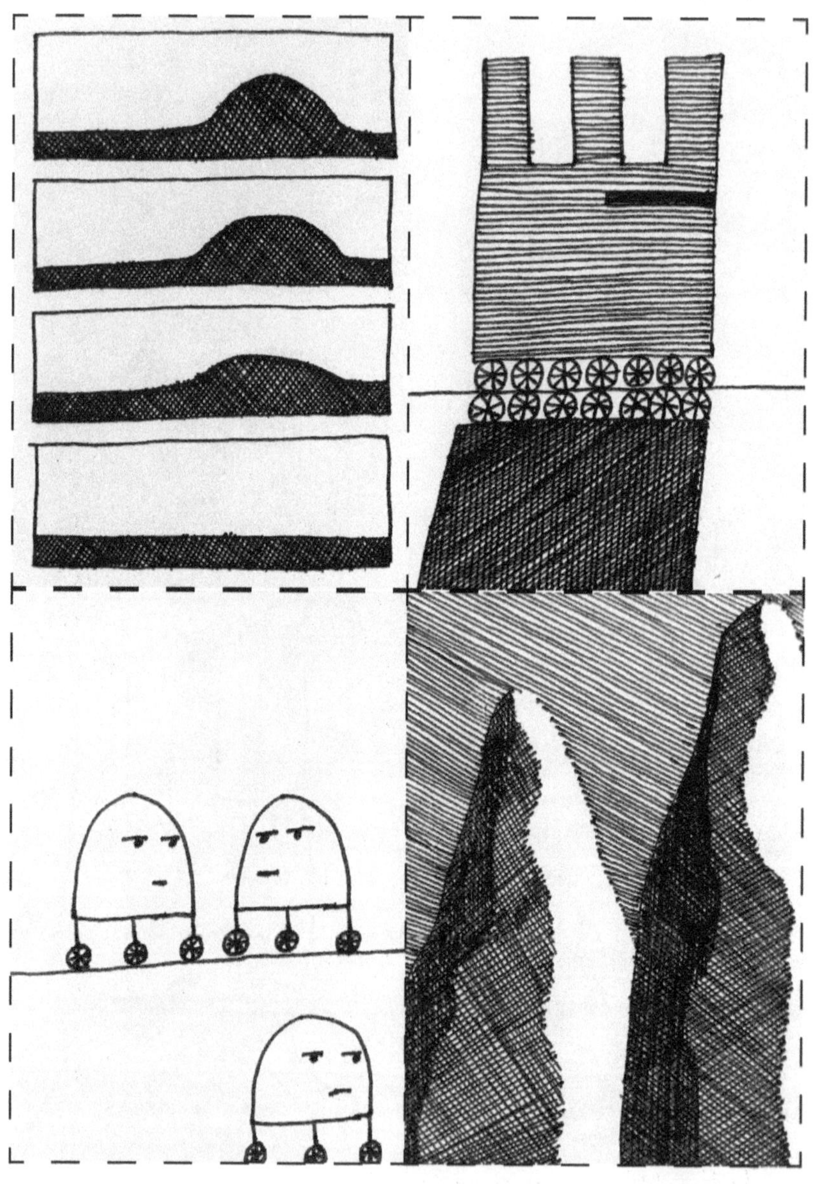

northern machines

northern machines

northern machines

Echolocation

by Karen Harris

When I was 13 and my parents were doing okay, we had a house with pillars. It was just a split-level ranch, but the pillars and our long sloping front lawn with apple trees created the impression of stateliness. Especially in the eyes of the gymnastics boys—city boys from Winthrop who dropped me off after a gymnastics meet one late afternoon. Oh, fancy. Wow, they said. Rich girl. I scoffed— proud, misunderstood, ashamed. I liked one of the boys. I said nothing. Just got out and ran as fast as I could around to the back door.

When my parents decided we could no longer afford that pillared house in the Massachusetts suburbs, we moved up to New Hampshire, just over the border to the town that's home to Canobie Lake Amusement Park. Our house was in a new development, a 5-acre rectangle carved out of the woods called Owl's Nest. One of the builders of its garrisons and capes, a man who smelled of fresh mulch and plaster, told people he'd spotted an owl when they were clearing trees. Just the one. When owls venture out alone, they're sometimes attacked by smaller birds, who are afraid of them. Despite the torment, though, the owls almost never get badly hurt.

I tried to like the new house, but I hated the cold, dark New Hampshire roads where I waited for the school bus in the mornings—my long, wet hair frozen into ropes—to take me to the regional high school miles away. Those first weeks at school, I cultivated a niche—new girl, mysterious and unknowable—and kept it up indefinitely. Floating between friend groups and ideas of myself seemed like an effective, if cowardly, strategy.

When summer came, I got a job spinning cotton candy at Canobie Lake Park. I worked in a sticky trance inside a hot closet-sized kiosk across from the kiddie boats. As a child, I'd loved everything about Canobie. The place had intoxicated me. We only went two or three times a summer, but I felt its narcotic pull every sunny day from May through September. At the end of each rare visit, after a day of rides and fried foods and sweets, I prayed that I would live there one day. Looking out our station wagon's back window, I would contract my diaphragm, hold my breath, and send a signal from my core up over the top of the ferris wheel to God. I'd have given anything. When we really did move to New Hampshire, I cursed this younger self for wishing it all into existence.

On breaks from the cotton candy hut, I walked around the park. I watched little kids pretend-pilot power boats in suspended circles above gray water. I wandered past the vintage merry-go-round and its re-glazed ponies with too-red lips. I stepped over trash: cigarette butts, discarded strings from candy necklaces, crumpled tickets, the occasional condom. I heard scraping wheels and screams, and steered clear of handsy boys and drunk down-and-outers. Pigeons scattered in front of me in fits and flights of fresh panic. I left my shift every night with a thin film of cotton candy covering my hair like a pink helmet, and tried to slip past my bosses after punching

out. They were all about 22 and seemed to be heavy pot smokers. I recognized a few as the older brothers of new high school friends.

One night years later, when I was about their age living in a drafty duplex in Boston after college, I went to a modern art thing down at the Cyclorama gallery with a new artist friend. Once inside, we stopped in front of a series of paintings on the wall—huge white canvases with giant concentric yellow circles. I shook my head and said too-easy things. This is bullshit. Just circles? I don't get it. I could do that. My friend laughed. Yeah, but you didn't.

My father got fired from his job around that time. Probably something to do with his drinking. (My mother recently told me about the time a pint of vodka slid out from under his car seat and hit her in the ankle when she'd borrowed his car.) None of us—my siblings or my mother or me—confronted him about his drinking then. We all had our reasons. Mine were: he had a temper, he was proud, I loved him, and I thought I had more time. When he got hired back at half his former salary, he wore cardigans instead of suit jackets to work from then on. The cardigan rebellion. He spent most of his nights after that drinking Miller Lite and carving duck decoys—the folk-art kind for displaying on mantels, not the kind you use to fool real ducks to their death.

My parents moved from their Owl's Nest garrison into a much smaller house a few towns over, and then my father got sick. My mother kept working as an overnight nurse on maternity, and got a riding mower for their small lawn. When I came up from Boston to visit, she and I would sometimes drive by one of our old houses and park outside, a few cars down. We'd sit there looking at the house, then she'd say "Okay?" and we'd drive on to the next house, or to her current one with the riding mower and my dying dad and his decoys.

I began dating a well-known actor. He lived on a big spread in upstate New York. When he was courting me, he said he wanted to meet my family and see where I "came from." I had no intention of taking him to that house, which was fine, because he had no intention of ever going there. I thought years later about how lonely he'd seemed, just one man on that big spread, making promises.

Funny, because shortly after that, I moved in and started housesitting for a wealthy friend in a mansion with a full-time gardener who'd worked there since my friend was a small girl. It was such a huge house, and I felt ridiculous staying there. I often woke up and didn't know where I was. And even living for free, I went into debt, having developed a habit of spending money—mostly on clothes and eating at restaurants—just to get out of the house. When a boyfriend wondered aloud over dinner one night why I always seemed poised to run, I pretended not to hear. The day I moved out, I was approaching my car in the driveway carrying a heavy box of cassettes when I saw a giant blue heron on the roof of my car just standing there, regal and still. The gardener and I watched it fly away in its prehistoric, slow motion way. "They're monogamous, you know," he said.

Years later, I started dating a man nine years younger than I who seemed steady and beautiful. It was a nice surprise—the whole thing. We had a baby, then married. Then another baby. In between babies, we bought a house—an 1885 farmhouse with a big yard. The family who lived there before us had raised six kids in that house, and they'd never lived anywhere else. I learned about nesting, and I nested. I started gardening.

When the kids were little, we visited a friend's goat farm in Vermont. My toddler son fell into a cistern that was six feet deep, but it was dusk and it looked like the earth had swallowed him. We heard a splash, and I tried to go into the hole head first. My husband and his friend pulled me out by the legs and my husband jumped in. I heard my boy crying. My husband handed him up to me, his winter jacket and snow pants soaked through from the whey water at the bottom of the cistern.

The couple who lived on the farm a half-mile away came to check on us; they'd heard our screams and raced over. The scene of them pulling up the gravel driveway in their pickup truck made me think of an article I'd recently read about how dolphins and bats use echolocation to send signals to one another, sometimes over vast distances.

The woman in the couple was a volunteer EMT. She started examining my son, then looked up and noticed my daughter, who was four, running nervously in place up on the porch, clapping her little fists together. I ran over, scooped her up, and brought her to her brother. The woman calmed her down by having her listen through the stethoscope to the beating heart under my son's wet shirt. See? Hear that? He's okay. It struck me as the perfect thing to do.

I sat on our friends' porch holding and rocking my son, who was bundled in my husband's jacket and a wool blanket as we waited for his snowsuit to dry in the dryer. I'd never felt so many versions of desperate at the same time as I did on that porch holding his warm, rescued body. I buried my face in his damp blonde hair and thought about the sending out of signals—animal to animal, person to person. Signals of thanks. Signals of warning and fear. Signals of presence.

I imagined the pins of all my places on a map, and the threads connecting them. Flight patterns. I thought about my dead father and how in my dreams he's always wearing a cardigan and jeans. I watched the stars come in, one by one. I thought about the yellow concentric circles on those giant canvases, and understood 20 years late that they were saying, quieter then louder, again and again: *Are you there? Are you in there? I'm here. In here.*

Intensive Care

by Michael Salcman

No figures here but pulse, breath and pressure;
no metonymy of fate but a real hand
cold upon a real sheet.
What could any actor speak more piercing
than this: the dull passage of the day, steady
in its silent leaking through a valve,
passing without acknowledgement,
without an eye-blink or a wave,
just the constant beeping, the mechanics
of death in a noisy room
seven stages above the street
with its rooms full of obdurate facts.
where life once made its living.

Simple Math

by Pamela Painter

The bruised red pickup from the last three weeks meanders up alongside the pumps where I'm stacking oil cans and dodging the night's slow-moving moths. There's a chill in the air and soon I'm going to look for my sweater, though Calley, the girl I alternate shifts with, says the owner likes us girls to show a little flesh. Early on, I voiced amazement to her that so many townspeople came way out here for gas, nine cents more than town.

"Not people," she said. "Didn't you notice how many dudes come by for our high-priced gas. Guys. Old guys. Harmless husbands."

She's an hourglass from halter tops to ample hips. Glossy curls. She stuck out her chest and winked at me. It's true. We get nice tips when guys like the way we lean across to swipe their windshields, open their hoods to lean in and check their oil.

And just like she said, the driver of the pickup, the guy with a red bandana around his forehead, once again sits there squinting beady eyes at me. He wants me to remember him. I don't give him that honor, and add three more cans to my oil can tower. Finally he calls, "Hey, Doll, good seeing you again too. Now, can you pump me four dollars worth?"

It takes me thirty seconds, nozzle in and out, and I'm standing beside his window.

He arches up his skinny torso, legs straight, to scrabble around in his front pocket. Grinning, he goes to hand over a hundred-dollar bill, but it drops to the oily pavement, just like it was planned. I bend to pick it up, knowing what I let him see of me. Hoping it's enough.

"You don't have something smaller," I ask, thinking the too-easy thought that sure he does, in more ways than one. "How about a credit card."

His large head swivels my way. Still grinning. "Nope. Nothing smaller, Doll," he says. "Not one damn thing."

On my way to deal with our old cash register I call out really loud, "Hey Jeb, middle pump hose is feeling squirrelly. It might need looking into." Jeb isn't here. He's off with his kid at little league. So of course, no Jeb appears to check the hose. I shrug as if Jeb answered me and glance at the pickup. Sure enough, pickup dude winks to show he's not been fooled.

I ding the register open and take my sweet time in getting him his ninety-six dollars in change, hoping another car will come along before I have to go back out there. First I slip out limp dollar bills till I get to the end of ones at 37. Before I start on fives I swish twelve quarters out of the trough. I'm good at math, though now in my senior year it's advanced trig.

There's a long beep of the pickup's horn to prove it works. His right arm is hanging limp out the window. Dangling down.

This is where, if Calley was working my shift, she'd be calling her boyfriend to drop by, his shotgun riding his gun rack like a trophy. Calley works the times when I'm looking after my grandma Lily till Uncle Earl comes home. Gram likes to hear about my

life. School. Classes. Awards. She has big plans for me, always has, which is why I have big plans. It's simple math. I make Grandma Jello almost every day. Her favorite flavor is cherry. There are red dots on all her clothes.

With the quarters cupped in my palm, I'm at 40 dollars now and ready for fives. Dimes are tempting, but I don't want to stand there beside bandana-man's window counting dimes into his sweaty hand. The horn again.

College says I have to work for tuition, and I'll be glad to leave this gas station job behind. Mostly I'll be working in the cafeteria, wiping down chairs, hoping for no food fights, "keeping the cash registers honest" they said, once they heard about this job.

I'm still on fives when pickup dude calls, "Hey babe, you need me to help you count." His door squeaks open and clunks shut and now he's leaning back against his truck, thumbs tucked into the frayed pockets of his jeans. What the hell? This is the first time he's crawled out of his truck.

I reach for Jeb's gun from behind the rack of candy bars and chips. Tuck it into the back of my jeans. When I got hired Jeb said, "Use it if you have to. That gun ain't here for looks." I sling the register shut and turn around. It is fate.

Later that evening, before I start on homework, I tell grandma how it felt–the solid weight of the gun in the small of my back. Her spoon pauses, and a lump of Jello shivers waiting, her eyes glint. My grandmother is all ears for anything I have to tell, and I know from stories that both she and my grandpa were hell-raisers. Him raising a few skirts here and there till her shotgun kept him home. And his stories of her lucrative liquor business don't leave her coming off like any saint. I suspect I take after her.

I give her a second helping of Jello as I describe how, after I was done counting ninety-three dollars in bills, three in quarters, it felt like I was carrying a green bouquet out to that pickup. The dude was still leaning against his driver's door, exactly my height. He was grinning like a fish.

"So, I'm almost to the pumps when I drop the quarters on the oily pavement."

"Oh no," Grandma says. Her spoon jabs the Jello.

"Yep." But I tell her I dropped them on purpose. I describe how they spun around and around and finally twizzled to a dead stop. Grandma is grinning and nodding now as I tell her of course I had to pick them up. I had to bend low and I guess my blouse sort of billowed out as I scrabbled in the dirt for those quarters. She says, "I'll bet you stooped just low enough for him to see the gun tucked into your jeans. "

I tell her he said, "Whoa, Doll," holding up both hands. "Forget about the quarters."

"You got him," Grandma says.

I say, "He was back in his pickup like a rabbit diving into a hole." Then I describe how, being honest, I tossed the ninety-six dollars through his open window as he was turning the key. Then I backed up fast as his tires spun out leaving me and his quarters behind.

"I hope you picked up those quarters," grandma said. "Them's quarters for your college." I had to scrub my nails hard, but I told her yes.

I'm Trying to be a Person

by Rachel Abramowitz

on whom nothing is lost. I have ruined several custards with
    scalding impatience.
Not a good cry, or a bad cry, or a cry for this teacup

that holds—so gently!—everyone in space so there is time
    to cry. When something is lost, only that something

knows where it is, even if it comes back silent as an uncut page.

Forgive me for thinking
    I should not have to bear lost buttons, earrings, mittens, children.

What if I cannot keep
    things in orbit? If I cannot slow the fury

that spins things away from me, in all dimensions,
    so that the carrot forced from the tar-black soil offers up

a golden ring encircling the root—

Let's (not) Talk about Sex

by Lindsey Byars

My girls were seven and three when we decided to raise chickens. It was a group effort until the moment the cute phase was over and the hen party became more like a work camp; then the kids were done.

"I miss the chicks when they were little. Can we have more next year?" my oldest begged while we were in the car one day.

After four months, I was done with chicken shit and chasing the birds out of my neighbor's yard. I swallowed the "hell no" bouncing on the tip of my tongue and opted for a softer explanation that babies always get bigger, and that the six chickens we had were probably enough.

"But we have eggs," my three-year old insisted. "Won't those be babies?"

"Uh, no. We don't have a rooster."

From the rearview mirror, I could see the gears moving in my oldest child's head.

"What does a rooster have to do with baby chickens?"

I felt a prickle of sweat break out across my forehead as I tried to keep our car between the lines, bracing myself for the parenting pile-up ahead.

"Well, see, you need a girl and a boy to make a baby. It's the same with chickens."

"Why?"

In that moment, all I wanted to do was fly the coop.

"Um, our bodies are made special…and….ugh…"

"Never mind. I don't want to talk about it," my oldest child said, pumping the breaks on a conversation she could sense was about to be awkward.

Thank Christ, because I didn't want to talk about it either. But there it was, a flashing parent hazard alert, and I knew that my own chicks were growing. Whether I wanted to have it or not, this conversation was coming.

I am not, despite my Baptist upbringing and the fact my husband and I are raising children in the heart of the Bible belt, what you would consider conservative when it comes to my views on sex. I'm the first to condemn abstinence-only education. I begged the principal of the high school where I teach to let me have a seminar with all the girls on masturbation, which I was certain would probably improve the astronomically high pregnancy rate when girls figured out toys could do way more than teenage boys ever dreamed of (he did not approve this plan, nor did he appreciate my idea).

My students come to me with pregnancy scares and for advice about relationships. I'm the teacher they tell before their parents that they're gay, and the one they come to when they really aren't sure. My students know I won't judge them; they know I'll just listen. When I found out I had a group of freshmen girls blowing their way through the football team because "that's not sex,"

I proclaimed to an entire ninth grade class, "It's your face! What's more intimate than letting someone penetrate your face?!"

And yet here I was, completely terrified of saying "the s-word" with my own little women.

I wanted to listen to anything they needed to tell me with no judgement, but I didn't know if I was prepared to handle what they might say. These children were mine. I wanted them to respect and understand their bodies. As they matured into young women, I wanted my daughters to be confident in their sexuality without feeling the need to be validated by their peers. I wanted them to choose their partners selectively, and the more I thought about my maturing girls, the more I wanted them to remain far away from intercourse or genital encounters of any kind! I was screwed.

I did what any (writer) mother would do: I immediately looked for a book. Surely there would be magic words from actual experts that could appropriately convey the right message about sex to my children. There are about a million different results for different audiences and ages. How much information does a seven-year-old really need about this?

My own mother went for the NOVA video – educational and informative. The narrator was British, or at least he was in my mind. Important, foreign subjects must be told to the audience by important, foreign men. Or Tom Brokaw. I remember sex being described as "The Dance of Life," illustrated by some lovely shadow figures dancing and intertwining. I felt certain there was more to sex than that, but I was in dance classes back then, so I was confident I could manage. But then the NOVA video ended with a graphic shot of live childbirth, killing any desire I may have had to have sex or unprotected modern dance. Birth was more terrifying than anything Stephen King was dreaming up. "It" was no longer in my nightmares; a hairy watermelon forcing itself out of my vagina took

center stage. Surely I could do this sex talk thing better than a video, right?

Reading book review after book review, I began to rethink my own mother's approach. There were too many choices. One parent would rave about a book's presentation of the birds and bees while another was in horror at the content, insistent it was inappropriate to give so much information about sex to children. How much was too much? I considered skipping the how-to and going straight for the birthing video, maybe tossing in graphic pictures of genital warts for extra deterrence, but did I really want to scar my children? I began to ponder opening an Etsy store for chastity belts.

Since I couldn't even craft a cotton ball lamb in Sunday school, I focused my search on children's books. The results finally matched my comfort level. One book looked like any other kid's book— illustrated and featuring a fun bird as the main character—but this time our protagonist was a tour guide through the reproductive process. *It's So Amazing! A Book about Eggs, Sperm, Birth, Babies, and Families* for age seven and up. It was perfect, age appropriate, and better than a video. I placed the chosen one into my cart and checked out.

I had a plan now. I felt good about it! Until the book arrived.

Flipping through the pages, I made it to chapter four ("Growing Up") where there was a whole page of illustrations of naked people from infant to elderly. Old, saggy, less hair down there illustrations. "How long before that happens?" I wondered with a small amount of horror, instantly feeling like I should be having more sex before time runs out. Before I could digress any further, I continued into the book, glancing through sperm and eggs, but stopping short at chapter nine ("What's sex?"). This was the big question that my daughter needed answered, so I read each word to myself, imagining my voice reading them to my oldest:

"When a woman and a man want to make a baby, they hug and cuddle and kiss and feel very loving, and get very close to each other – so close that the man's penis goes inside the woman's vagina..."

My baby was seven! She picked her nose and played with Barbies! I put the book promptly in my underwear drawer, one more secret for Victoria to keep. I started thinking about Etsy again. I could learn to sew.

Avoidance worked well for a few months... Until the drive home from school one day several months later:

"Sam was chasing us and we couldn't make him leave us alone and he kept saying bad words...you know...like the s-word..."

"You've heard me say *shit* a million times."

"No, Mom. The *other* s-word..."

"What are you talking about?" I was fluent in sailor speak, so mentally I went down the list to find another word as we pulled into the driveway.

Frustrated with my ignorance, she unbuckled, climbed forward, and whispered low enough so her younger sister couldn't hear, "*Sex*, Mom."

Ready or not, I couldn't keep some little shit from sharing information with my innocent child. It was time.

I pulled *It's So Amazing* out from hiding one summer morning. I laid it ceremoniously into the center of my neatly made bed and tried to formulate a plan. Periods, sperm, and babies, oh, my.

My now eight-year-old (I really had procrastinated on having the talk) was up early that morning, and so we folded laundry and I tried to figure out how to dive in. She knew boys had a penis and girls didn't. My kids attended a small daycare, and when diapers were changed and everybody was learning how to use the potty, differences were established early on. I decided that perhaps the egg should come first, before the cuddling cocks and hens.

"The sperm has to reach the egg before a baby can happen," I explained as I folded towels and pointed to the illustrations in the book. We were both still in our pajamas, casual. No formalities. I could have won an Emmy for my performance, despite the slow death I was feeling inside. This was such a monumental milestone for me as a parent, marking an end to part of my child's innocence. I didn't want her to feel any pressure, so I kept my face relaxed and my tone calm.

"Our bodies are like puzzles that fit together, and that's how the sperm gets to that egg. But we don't always want a baby, so we can do things to keep the sperm and egg apart."

She didn't say anything, but looked deep in thought as the gears clicked and turned. I continued.

"Remember the medicine I take to keep me from having another baby?" Birth control we had covered in the CVS pharmacy line the year before. "That keeps the egg from coming into the tube, which keeps the sperm from getting to an egg."

"Oh. I get it." She was keeping her cool, too. My first-born child was contemplative. She would need time to process before really asking questions, but this was a start.

I told my daughter about different kinds of love, and that sex can be a way we show love to special people, but I let the statement hang there without much explanation. How do you define "special people" without opening an entirely new box of parental horrors? Just because you think someone is special doesn't mean they feel the same way about you. What should you do when people want to touch you but you don't want them to? What if that person is a teacher or other adult? I didn't want to scare her, but she needed to know that nobody has a right to touch her without her permission, so I told her that any touch that made her uncomfortable was not ok, and that she should tell them to stop. That included adults. I told her never to be behind a closed door with an adult, unable to keep myself from going to worst case scenario in my mind.

"But what if I get in trouble?" she asked. My child was a people pleaser who thrived on praise from authority figures. It was a quality that terrified me in this particular conversation.

"You stand in the hallway and tell them to call your mother, and you don't move until they do." The very thought made me nauseous, and I struggled with the images my imagination was conjuring.

"And I won't be in trouble?"

"Never. You will never be in trouble for standing up for yourself, no matter what they say."

Good and bad touches had been discussed in school. She understood what I was trying to communicate without an in-depth explanation of exactly what an adult might do and why I wouldn't want her alone with anyone, even a teacher. There was such a fine line between biology, love, pleasure, and abuse. I was tripping all over it, fumbling with what she needed to know and what she would figure out in the natural course of her life.

Through the course of our morning talk, we covered the science and general idea that sex is a way two people can show love to each other, but I resisted the urge to mount the "when you're married" pedestal of my youth, since I sure didn't. I didn't tell her to save herself for that one special man like my mother told me, but I also didn't go into a feminist lecture. Just the basics, no politics.

As I tried to navigate what was important to discuss at this phase of life, a few things became abundantly clear:

1. Eight-year-olds just need their questions answered.

2. My kids need to know that we can talk about anything.

3. And, to my mortification, I realized that this was the just the first of many sex talks to come.

Our bodies as puzzles isn't going to make as much sense when she starts asking about her best friend who has two moms, or when she catches on that sex isn't only for making babies or only done between people in love. I'll again have to decide how much my child needs to know, when it's appropriate to tell her more, and how we'll approach her sex life as she begins dating. Maybe by the time I have to talk about sex with her sister, I'll be better at this.

For our first conversation though, I thought I handled myself pretty well. I closed the book, pushed the laundry aside, and hugged my first born tightly, easing the tension I was holding in my chest. I could still pick her up, so I did. I told her she could ask me anything. I would always answer her questions, and if I didn't have the answer right away, I would help her find it.

"Or I can just Google it, right, Mom?"

"No! No Googling this. Just ask me anything."

His Grandma Blues

by Khem K. Aryal

His grandma is angry. His grandma is angry because he's hungry. She bluntly expresses her wish to cut him into two in a single stroke of a *khurpa*. Her hands scrabble on the semi-dark kitchen floor, around her feet partly covered by her sari, as if looking for a *khurpa*. To cut him into two in a single stroke.

She is fishing for firewood beside the oven, now dead. Anger makes it hard for her to concentrate. And it's getting dark. The sun has almost set, and there's no electricity. It's not time yet to light the kerosene lamp; darkness has to get thicker for the luxury. Once she kindles fire, a flickering light will paint the dark corner of the thatched-roofed house, displaying his grandma's bitter face and watery eyes. He's not sure if he wants to see it all. He is hungry and his grandma's angry face will make him feel more pathetic.

Now his grandma's anger has peaked because he is not just hungry, he's crying too. And there's not much she can do. She can prepare him cornbread that she knows he hates, he hates it because there won't be anything to go with it, like vegetable or yogurt. She can roast him dry corn and he always revolts against the idea of roasted dry corn. Dry and hard and it won't fill his stomach.

He's just returned from school, some fifteen minutes walk home. He hasn't had a thing to swallow since he had plain rice with a quarter bowl of milk around nine this morning. He is hungry and he faults his grandma for not having something ready for him to eat when he returns from school, while she keeps working her hands, not finding a thing, not kindling fire, but repeating profanity—she wants to cut him into two pieces. With a *khurpa,* the biggest sickle in the house, in a single stroke.

He knows she won't harm him. She hasn't ever touched him in the form of punishment. She doesn't have the guts to do it even if she's wild. He suspects she is this much angry and says she wants to cut him into two also because she can't punish him physically. She is a weakling. Or else, she has a special affection for him that she can't quite see because it's hidden behind the darkness of her bitterness.

But her anger hurts him. The rage she exhumes is painful to take in. He cries more. Now not just because of hunger but because of the intensity of hatred that he sees consuming her. His grandma doesn't express her wish to behead him when she has something to put in front of him upon his return from school, a tired and hungry nine-year-old. She simply tosses food to him and walks out. She doesn't talk. She doesn't ask him how his day at school was. She doesn't ask him how he's feeling. She doesn't know how to show her love for a nine-year-old, or anyone for that matter. She only gets angry when he is hungry. Sometimes he falls asleep while crying beside the oven, waiting for food. When he wakes up, he finds his grandma lost in thoughts.

His grandma is a widow. She has been a widow since he knew her. It didn't occur to him for a long time she could have a husband too, like grandmas of his playmates, and she'd lost him. But now he suspects that she is angry also because she is lonely. She never talks with him about his grandpa. But sometimes she is feeding him beside the oven, and her eyes fill with tears. She kneads her feet with a hand and makes tears with her eyes. He feels bad for her and thinks of his grandpa at such moments.

His grandma had two sons but only one survives. When he was born, his pa was in India, where he worked, and when he came home for a visit, he didn't stay long enough for him to know the man as his father. He's heard that his uncle died of unidentified causes in India. He has heard the village women say the younger son was his grandma's favorite. He was gentler, and came home for a visit from India every year. The last time he came, he is told, he played with the less-than-a year-old baby the whole time he stayed home. He returned to his wife and children in India in a month, and never came back.

His grandma has two daughters. Sometimes they come to visit her, usually during festivals and she spends most of her time listening to them, her eyes wet. When she talks in their presence, she talks loudly and laughs riotously, something she doesn't do with his ma. She often talks about relations. She knows who is who to whom in all the surrounding villages. She is animated when people start disentangling relations. He wishes her daughters visited her more. She is less angry when her daughters are around.

He believes his grandma is angry with his ma too, but he doesn't know the reason. Maybe his ma is mean to her. He doesn't know. In fact, he hardly knows his ma. He shares his bed with his grandma, and his grandma feeds him. His ma works outside, meaning that she tends the buffaloes, and she works in the field. She gets out in early morning to fetch fodder for the cattle. When she returns in the afternoon, he's gone to school. When he returns from school, she's still in the field. By the time she returns home, it's already dark— there's no electricity, and he can't see her very well.

She doesn't ask him about his day. She hardly asks him anything, in fact. She is busy. She works hard, from five in the morning to ten or eleven at night. He hears her cleaning dishes from his bed. He has rarely seen his grandma talk to her. If he asks her anything about his ma, she is angry.

His grandma is a scavenger by nature. He doesn't know much about what lies on the upper floor of the house. The floor's always dark—it has no windows, and everything in there is layered with soot that rises from the kitchen downstairs. He likes it though when his grandma climbs up the stairs and starts rummaging through the darkness. She spends quite a while under the thatched roof, and sometimes comes down with a piece of coconut or a sugar candy for him. When she hands him the treasure, she says nothing. She only sticks her hand out to him, her find still hiding in her closed fist.

The gift is so treasured. It can't be even called by a name. It can't be openly displayed. He has to grab it from her hand and put it into his mouth in a flash. He has to close his mouth tightly and swallow the morsel secretly. As if an invisible creature would otherwise grow envious and snatch it. She is especially cautious when his ma happens to be around, though she does most of her scavenging when she's alone.

During the monsoon season, when mangoes ripen, her first job in the morning is to rummage the bushes in the mango groves. She wants to make sure that she gets the best of the windfall. In fact, she wants all the mangoes. Good or bad. She's usually back when he's awake but not out of his bed yet. She sits beside him and sees him eat some, while she keeps for herself the ones that don't look good, mostly the ones with holes in them. She doesn't care about worms. She is angry if he complains. There are no bad mangoes.

After mangoes come guavas. She cannot climb trees and guavas do not fall overnight like mangoes. Still, she visits the groves in early morning, and she is happy to collect a few bird-caved ones. She says the ones that the birds have tried taste better. She has no teeth, not a single one, so she cannot bite. The guavas are mostly for him, but she saves for herself the ones that are creamy-yellow-ish and that she can squeeze between her fingers. She doesn't care about the reddish slime blotting her clothes. She is angry if his ma complains about it. She enters a soliloquy that she'll wash her own clothes.

His grandma has developed an unmatched love for the fruit of *khaniyo*, a kind of wild fig. It's not fruit for most villagers. The fruits that are on the vines don't have as much flesh as the ones that are on the roots, neither buried nor fully out in the open. His grandma knows exactly where the fleshy ones are to be found. When he's home from school, the fruits are the first thing she offers him if she happens to have them during the season. But his ma is not happy with the way his grandma practices poverty. She believes they are not as poor as his grandma projects it to be by collecting wild fruits. He has never heard his ma talk about eating them. He imagines that her relationship with *khaniyo* ends with its foliage that she collects to feed buffaloes. They have good enough land to produce corn and millet to last for the whole year. They also have a small paddy field though the rice it yields is not enough for them, and so they're forced to eat corn meal that they all hate. His grandma wants to believe that they have no paddy field at all; they have no buffaloes to supply them milk; they have nothing in the house. They are poor. Very very poor. That's why her son is forced to be a *muglani*, a migrant worker. That's why she lost one of her sons.

There are rumors that his uncle was killed. What a karma he didn't get to die a natural death! He was killed in *muglan*, a foreign land, like a stray dog. For reasons no one knows. There are rumors still circulating that it had to do with his marriage. But who knows? What killed the father of two young daughters? His grieving grandma will never know. She won't get anybody to help her find out the reason. The other son is useless at it. He isn't even home in times of her sorrow. What is she left with but a hole in her heart and an uncertain longing to know what killed the poor man who never quarreled with a villager or any family member.

He is told his grandma loves him most because he came to this earth to fill the vacuum his uncle would soon leave. She hasn't told him anything about her lost son, but she has uttered a couple of times in a muffled voice "loved you." She doesn't even say who loved him. When she says this, tears well in her eyes and she chokes.

He's still hungry and he's crying. Even if she kindles fire now and starts cooking something, it'll take time to be ready. He's in no condition to wait. He's pathetically hungry. He begins to cry more as he thinks that his grandma must have spent the whole afternoon going around the village, probably disparaging his ma. She extracts pleasure from disparaging family members, he knows, but he also knows that the very act makes her unhappier when she goes to bed. Is that why her pillow is a tear-stained mess?

She expresses her wish again to neatly cut him into two pieces. With a sharp *khurpa*, a *khurpa* that the villagers use to slaughter goats in Dashain. He has digested her threat, but her madness tortures him. He is devastated. He cries more.

"*Khurpale chhapakka dui tukra parera,*" neatly into two pieces with a *khurpa*. "*Dushman!*" she says. *Dushman*, the enemy! She wants to cut her enemy into two pieces.

He suddenly understands that his grandma has enemies, enemies that she wants to cut into two pieces. His grandma is angry, but not with him. He pauses his crying.

"*Dushman,*" she repeats. "They killed my *babu*," my baby son! She can't locate any firewood; she doesn't seem to be searching for it anymore. She's searching for a *khurpa*. A *khurpa* to cut her enemy into two pieces, the enemy who killed her son who'd been forced to flee to India in search of work.

He stops crying. He does not feel hungry anymore. Or else, he doesn't want to eat anything although he's hungry. Or, he may eat anything his grandma might toss his way. Or, not eat at all if his grandma chooses not to prepare him anything. His grandma is angry, angry and sad and helpless.

He's filled with what feels like pity for her. There is no soul more miserable than a soul helplessly angry and sad. He thinks of grabbing her hand and commanding her to stop pretending that she's searching for firewood. He wants her to stop the nonsense and confront him instead— What's your selfish hunger in front of my soul-crushing sorrows? Stop whining and become a man! But he cannot. He's not used to showing concern for anyone openly. He's not used to showing his love or having love shown to him publicly. The most they can do to show love in his family is to cry. It is intensely primordial and degrading but that's what they do.

But he doesn't even want to cry for his grandma. He doesn't feel so intense yet to show his love.

He is exhausted, and his grandma has started kneading her feet in the thickening dark. They have nothing to talk about, or to complain. They have both gone through their own struggles and lost them in their own ways. They will accept their fates, at least until he returns home from school yet another day to no snacks ready for him and his grandma is again overcome by the loss of her favorite son.

Three Poems

by Adam Fell

BEHOLDER

I watch the sun set through the torn ear of a dead rabbit / delicate paws tangled in bright grass / little star / once bolting / now a maze of wilting fur / neck snapped by a happy dog near the back-stop fence // Together / we are time tilting forward too perceptibly to ignore // Together, our bodies unravel / bright veins collapsing / bouquets of white extinction in a world of green abundance // Aching / adrift / aseptic / grazing the air / like the ashes of mad cattle we had to burn because we fed them the flesh of their own dead //

COLLUSION

Outside / our kids make sleeping bags of the gentle dark's more intricate muscles // Their blood / a thousand falling satellites / their eyelashes fogged by the raid-light of our ever-rising rent // They sneak smokes among the glassy remains of our pharmacological record / inhale a minty poison syrup / dance inside the lingering magic of undaunted contraceptives // Each morning their throats beg for clarity & awe / they paw for potable water in a welt-blue dawn too beautiful to be good for their bodies // They will join us / soon / if we're not careful // The world will shake them too from its pelt like dust // We made of this beautiful place a wakeful blonde obscenity / dying yet unflushable / withered in our white corridors / a blotch of unbridled biases // We made of ourselves / devout explosions / who deserve to be damned //

LIFE AMONG REPRODUCTIONS

You are no better than the world you live in / is what I sing to you tonight // Don't take it personally // You will find love someday / seething screenface to seething screenface / we sit with each other / far away / together / in the mist of our mutual losses / ash-tagged & caked in aspartame / our seditious hearts rung up on rhabdo & rail margaritas / keychained to the luckless paws of rabbits that froze to death beneath the downspouts of our debased country // Ready or not / our home has nowhere left to live // All the streets here have patriotic names // We prowl the edges of our preserve / baby lions / dreaming of bloody muzzles while we wait for our jaws to react / long after the zebra has fled //

COVID Diaries

by Belle (Bom) Kim

COVID Diaries 02

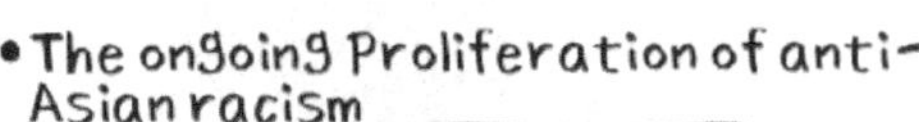

Self-Reflection

CURRENT MOOD

These Days

THESE DAYS...

I HAVEN'T BEEN ABLE TO FOCUS ON MUCH OF ANYTHIN

LA LA LA
LA LA LA
LA
LA

WHAT A TIME TO BE ALIVE.

The Way Things Are

by Susan Volchok

... And, in the spring—as soon as possible, when the ground was just warming, the snow melting down all the sewers and into the ponds and the reservoir, everything clean and wet and beginning to green—we went as often as we could to Central Park, especially on weekends. We had fallen in love in that park, of course, when I was in high school and he was my much older, wiser, handsome city friend. I met him every Sunday for a few hours, and I cried alone in the tunnel waiting for the train back to the suburbs, because we had such talks—lying on our backs on the hot, black lake-rocks, or walking, a little apart, not even touching hands usually, but just walking slowly along through the grass, over the concrete, into the remnants of pine forest—such talks that my heart began its growing pains, my chest was hurting with happiness and I never wanted to be done then. But we didn't know we were in love until I came back from school, and we looked at one another, sitting on the swings in the park that May, dangling our legs and laughing, and we looked at one another, and we stopped laughing for a moment and we knew.

So, naturally, we had a special sense of the place. And when we went there, from early spring through late autumn of every year, though it was for the pleasure of each particular day, it was in memory of the past as well. The park made us feel how strong we were together, how we had got on (such a long while, endless delays) and were still here. And then too, it was a sign of how surely we would continue: the park was also for the future.

But in the park, it was not the growing things, the new buildings, the polar bear turning fat and yellow in a rocky pool, that signified, or at least not for him. He was (suddenly, it seemed, but perhaps it was more gradual than I can recall) captivated and… inspired by the children. Hadn't they been there all along? But now he was seeing them as if for the first time. We would be strolling slowly hand in hand, talking or not, no particular destination, and suddenly he would cry, "Look!" and I would whirl around, expecting something miraculous, such excitement in his voice, and it would be a tiny, dark-haired child eating an ice cream cone. He was seeing them with new eyes, that much was clear, and asking me, without at first asking, to see them as he did.

They appeared in the playgrounds and in the worn meadows as early in the year as we: infants sleeping, crying in pink, wrapped in blue afghans, their streamlined grey-and-silver carriages pushed along the paths by nurses or grandmothers. Or toddlers in corduroy, red and yellow flashes running circles around their fathers, running away from their primly pretty, well-dressed mothers, who were not much bothering with them anyhow, huddling on the benches together as they did, talking about who knows what— their homes, I imagined, and their dogs and their husband's jobs and, of course, their children. It was mostly mothers there, even on weekends, and I watched them sometimes the way he watched the kids; only silently, and with a different feeling in the watching. I never wanted that, to sit there with the others in the bright air, on duty, to be stiffly responsible for the well-being of strange little charges, to forget, myself, how to play. I didn't want it, didn't want to be one of them; no, thank you, no.

And when, sometimes at night, he would say, "You know, I think now and then about our children, how they will be," I would only laugh and kiss him goodnight and turn as if to sleep. But there would be tears starting as I pressed my eyelids down hard (I never could stand crying, not even my own). They were angry tears: What was he trying to do to me? I knew it was really my place to say (later, much later) the sort of thing one had heard or read, something, something... such as "Oh, my darling, I do want to have your babies." And I did love him. But I was young, but I was going to disappoint him, but I would fail; I could feel it all then.

Bitter thoughts, and frightening. So that when, after a long time spent watching children in the park, he began to do more than marvel at this curly haired marbleshooter, or that towhead sailing a two-foot yacht... when he began turning to me once or twice each weekend, and asking "Aren't we ever going to?" anger and fear took the truth from my mouth. The easier thing was to smile fondly, foolishly, as if to say, Yes, soon, and finally, I did say "Soon."

Soon. Sooner than that, something else: a chance to go away, to live and study abroad. A chance to escape: I wanted to take it; no, I had to take it. I must have been longing and hoping for this opportunity, this exit; I must have been that scared out of my love. He cried. I cried, too, only because I had never seen a man cry before in my life. I cried for him. He decided to believe I couldn't leave him, and became calm. We didn't talk about it again, not for many months. But we didn't go to the park anymore either. We were waiting, each in our own way.

Then, one week, a new passport appeared on the bureau, in a new leather folder. And the next, a vaccination certificate, traveler's checks, a plane ticket. He said nothing, his eyes showed nothing either, they were black and cold. But he couldn't sleep, I knew that.

Late one night, he sat down in the rocking chair beside the bed and spoke to me. "You're always leaving; you think you can always come back. And maybe that was so in the past. But this is it: if you go this time, I won't be waiting here for you, not ever again. It's your choice. But if you're really going, we'll settle things now. Not your way, 'later.' No. There's no room in my later for you. If you go." And he rocked and rocked and rocked, and refused to cry or plead. Only, choose.

I had already chosen. I chose what I had to choose, the long good-bye, the last settling up, and a long, lonely year in industrious exile. I came home on the Fourth of July, the Statue of Liberty glowing in a haze beneath the plane, fireworks in the park, and steaming, cheering crowds at the airport. I picked up, put back together most of the pieces of the life I'd left behind. I worked and lived, I loved some men, and I made it, I made it without him. I never called to tell him I was back, never wrote, never sent any birthday or holiday messages. I would never see him again.

Never not for fifteen years. Yesterday. In the park, it was, and where else would I meet him but there? And yet, it's a kind of miracle, so unusual for me to go all the way across to the playground. We don't live as close as I once did, years ago. With him. And I don't much care for it now, that park.

But it was a beautiful morning, everything clean and sunwashed and so alive and green that it seemed a fine idea. I was pushing the stroller up the last path to the fenced-in asphalt where kids screamed and ran, their mothers turning their own polished faces to the sun. And he was coming down, cautiously, pulling back on the handle of a small, old-fashioned plaid summer carriage.

Of course, we stopped, and we shook hands, we held one another's hands for a long while, he looking down at my face and I...

I was looking at the ground. He knelt before the stroller and tousled the boy's dark hair, and I told him, "David; he's almost two and a half." Side by side, we gazed into the tight little face of the sleeping girl, and he told me her name: Sophie.

"She's three months old," he said. "We had lost one… it's more than three years ago."

"I'm sorry," I said. "But she must make you very happy; you must be very happy now."

We stood a little apart, then, awkward. So much to say, nothing whatever to say, so much, nothing…

"You're looking well," he said.

"You too," I answered.

There was another long silence between us. And the boy began kicking his feet against the pavement, wanting to move on. "Don't forget we have to meet Daddy, don't forget, don't forget, don't forget…."

"I haven't forgotten, Davie," I said. He was watching David so closely, thinking, perhaps, *He looks just like you…* thinking something I wanted to believe must be very sad, his mouth was drawn and trembling. And suddenly, I wished for some one simple thing to say to him, the very thing he would like to hear with all his heart. It would be my last chance. Turning toward him, meeting his serious stare, I said (very quietly and sadly, I wanted that, yes, but still, there was the trace of a smile), "It might have all been so different. And it might have been good; who knows?"

"You're crazy," he said, and he laughed, clear and careless and so easy. He was really laughing, as he walked around to the front of his baby's carriage again. Laughing. Free and easy. "It would have been terrible. You knew it then, before I did. You were right, and I was a fool. But everything's come out fine, that's what counts. We got our happy ending after all." He laughed again and pushed the carriage lightly abreast of the stroller, squeezed my arm as he smiled goodbye, moved on.

The boy was bouncing up and down in his seat, whining, "Daddy's waiting, come on, come on, come on," and I was watching the carriage disappear around the curve of hedge behind us. He never looked back, not even a glance, and I was thinking, *He is right and I am a fool; he's happy, I'm happy, everyone's happy after all…*

And, so much happiness, I began to cry standing in the hot sun in the middle of the uphill path. My little boy was frightened; his mother never, ever cries. I stopped then, and said "I'm crying, sweetie, but it's a special kind of crying, and it's our secret now, I'm telling you and nobody else." My sweet love. I wheeled him around, back out through the park. And oh, the sun, the leaves bursting in the air, the flowers pulsing in the new grass, kites hovering, sailboats skittering the ponds— what, no birds singing?

"Sing, Davie," I said. "Sing now, Going home to Daddy, going home to Daddy… sing louder. Going home, going home, going home to Daddy." Home, happiness. Home, happy end. Happy, happy day: sing, love.

Agnes Varda: The Ardent Background

by Cole Swensen

Always in the background of her films, landscape
as seeing
                        at times through a window
framed by a curtain
                        held back by a hand. Landscape
as that hand
                        held up to the sunlight
                        showing through.

Or landscape of a hand
                        reaching out
to take a box of matches
                        off a shelf
that sees itself strike a match
                        to light a candle at noon.

Candle that sees
                        because a flame is a living thing.
Landscape as all
                        that is living in the eye in range.
Landscape as living
                        in the range of an eye.

The past doesn't mean
                        so much to me because it's always here.

Scene of silence
                filling first the screen.
Scene of a hat
                walking away.
Scene white with sun
                      until she is sitting on a wall
in a field
                where the sun breaks down
                          because another sun
has come quietly in.

Bill Viola: The Reflecting Pool, 1977-79

by Cole Swensen

The pool and the faces of dark. The pool and what moves across
and a man climbs out and walks off.
And a man walks through a forest uncommonly green, a man walks
up to the stone wall that forms one end
of the reflecting pool, walks through the yellow-green foliage,
    made so
by the dense green's being fused with light
which lies across the top of the wall as he climbs up onto the wall
    and waits.
The yellow-green water with all the light on it
constantly changes or the reflection that is it
subtly evolves beneath the man who arcs out to leap in but remains
suspended against the background
of trees until he is inseparable from the leaves and we see
the reflections of unseen things.

Sphincters I Have Known and Lost

by Jon Shorr

"You want to hear about all the times I've had tubes shoved up my penis?"

There's a sentence I never thought I would ever speak or write to other people.

Until I got cancer.

When I was growing up my family never sat around the dinner table talking about death, politics, family secrets, our dates, personal insecurities, or anything serious, for that matter. There was never any talk of how Grandma died or whatever happened to Aunt Helen's first husband—or for that matter, the fact that Aunt Helen had had a first husband. There was certainly never any mention of the fact that in 1960, my older cousin Lucy had converted from Judaism to Catholicism, married a Black man, and moved with him back to his home in Kenya. In short, personal information, much less anything that might be considered embarrassing, was not for public consumption, at least in my family.

When I became a parent, I carried these practices into my own family. My kids learned early to avoid talk—at least with me—about topics that might make me squirmy. Even when I visited my daughter and her husband in Chicago after the birth of their first baby, she assured me that the only reason that her husband was sleeping in the bedroom with her was so that I could sleep on the couch in the living room, "where he usually sleeps, of course," she said.

As I said, that's who I was until I got cancer. Bladder cancer.

For some people, cancer defines the line of demarcation between feeling immortal and accepting their mortality. For some, it defines the line between barely noticing the daily bodily pains and twinges and the assumption that each of those twinges is the first sign of The Cancer That's Going to Kill Me. For me, cancer redefined the line between what I considered private and what I was willing to make public, that willingness to disclose personal details, that assumption that random strangers and acquaintances want to know the unpleasant and intimate details of my life. There were other costs of having had cancer, of course: physical, emotional, and financial. There was a new and continuing awareness of my mortality. There was some physical discomfort along the way. But that was the main one, forgetting that there's a line that separates the personal details I'm willing to make public and those I'm not.

I've taken enough psychology and interpersonal communication courses to know all about the trust-risk cycle, that you only disclose as much information as you think is safe, that will not cause rejection, embarrassment, or humiliation, and that as relationships develop, you're gradually willing to "risk" more, to disclose more personal information as you develop more trust in the other person.

And yet, I just ignored all that and shared with you, a total stranger, the fact that I've had countless tubes shoved up my penis.

I was driving home to Baltimore from Hershey, Pennsylvania, where I'd had dinner with my son Christopher. He was working for a company that gives hotels their ratings, was under cover reviewing a resort hotel, and needed a "dinner companion" to help not call attention to himself. After discussing the meal (presentation and taste were excellent, as was the wait staff's attentiveness, although the tablecloth had a stain on it, and the flowers at the maître d's station were a bit past their prime, as was the maître d'), Christopher went back to his room to evaluate the turn-down service, and I left for the hour-and-a-half drive back to Baltimore.

At some point I needed a bathroom stop. Urgently. Much more urgently than usual. I pulled into an old Texaco station off I-83 just south of the Pennsylvania line in Maryland, raced into the very dirty, smelly restroom, peed out a blood clot the size of Detroit, and realized that there was probably something very, very wrong.

Three days later, I screwed my courage to the wall and made myself tell my primary care doctor about peeing out that clot. Normally calm and unflappable, this doctor who'd been my physician for 20 years and whose standard response to any symptom I had was telling me to wait a few days to see if it got better on its own picked up his phone before I finished talking and made an appointment for me the next day with a urologist.

"You have bladder cancer," the urologist said, after looking at the inside of my bladder through a tube his tech had shoved up my penis.

These are the things that do it, I thought, the invasions of your personal space, the invasions of your body by total strangers. I know that women have dealt with this forever, gynecological exams by older men, for example, but it wasn't something I'd had to think about until I'd had a tube shoved up my penis.

"You're going to die," the urologist continued, bedside manner being his weak suit, "but it won't be from this." He went on to tell me not only that what I had was the most common kind of bladder cancer—information that was simultaneously reassuring and not—and that it was Stage T-a, which meant that it was confined to the bladder lining (the epithelium) but had not yet moved into the muscle of the bladder. The good news, he said, was that it was slow-growing and easily treatable; the bad news was that it was likely to recur.

A week later, I was back in the outpatient procedure suite of his office to have the tumor scraped off by instruments that the urologist manipulated through an even bigger tube that one of his techs shoved up my penis. "That's what we'll do first," Jaz said. Everyone in the office called my urologist "Jaz," I assumed because it was a shortened version of his last name, but maybe (I found out later) because he was also a jazz pianist in his spare time. "We'll scrape it off and send you home with a Foley catheter," he said.

I immediately flashed to Foley artists, the sound effects people who walk and run in Foley Pits to create movie and television characters' footsteps: high heels clicking on a tile floor, Nikes running down a sticky asphalt alley on a hot summer night. Maybe in addition to the Foley Box, I thought, Jack Foley, the sound effects technician in the early days of talking films after whom Foley artists and Foley pits are named, had also invented the Foley Catheter, used to recreate screams of pain and terror. In fact, the Foley catheter, a device for draining urine, blood, and other disgusting fluids from your bladder when it's unable to do that on its own, was named for Frederic Foley who designed the contraption in 1929.

"Does that mean I won't be able to go out while I have the catheter in?" I asked.

"No, do whatever you want," the doctor said. "You just need to wear sweats or some other kind of loose-fitting pants to accommodate the urine-collecting bag that'll be strapped to your leg. After two or three days," he said, "when you don't see any blood in your urine, that'll mean that your bladder's healed enough that you can remove the catheter and collection bag."

I wasn't a sweat pants kind of guy. I wasn't athletic. I grew up in the 60s. I wore khakis, button-down shirts, and ties at work and jeans the rest of the time.

"Why are you wearing sweats?" my friends and colleagues asked me that first time. What should I say? Should I lie? But what would the lie be? I'm a terrible liar, anyway.

"I had a little medical thing Friday," I said, "and I have to wear loose-fitting pants for a few days."

By the third time I'd been scoped and scraped, though, it was just part of who I was. "I had a tumor scraped off the inside of my bladder, and I have to wear a pee bag for a few days until it's healed." I noticed that people gave me a little extra space then, not wanting to risk bumping my leg and causing who-knows-what to happen.

That was the beginning of the treatment, scraping the cancer cells out of my bladder. The second phase, which started a week or so after that, was trying to keep them from returning. That consisted of periodically squirting BCG into my bladder. BCG stands for "Bacillus Calmette Guerin," which is a classy way of saying Bovine Tuberculosis, which someone figured out can kill bladder cancer cells. The good news about BCG is that unlike regular chemo, it's bladder-specific rather than systemic, which means that its side effects don't affect your other body parts: you don't get nausea or hair loss, for example. The bad news is that there are bladder-specific side effects, mainly irritation, inflammation, scarring, a craving for alfalfa, and most noticeably, spasms.

So, what's wrong with a few bladder spasms? Nothing, except that every time your bladder spazzes, it contracts and makes you have to pee. And as the treatments went on and my bladder got more irritated ("it looks like a bomb went off in there!" Jaz said one day after scoping me out during one of my regular office visits, making small talk and trying unsuccessfully to reassure me about something or other), the spasms became more frequent.

I carried an empty milk jug in the car to pee into if I couldn't make it to a gas station in time. On one trip, I drove with my fly open, peeing fairly regularly into my milk jug, hoping that traffic would slow down and at the same time hoping that someone in an SUV or truck wouldn't pull up next to me and look down through my car's window to see what I was doing. I had my classes moved to rooms closer to the men's room, so I could get there and back as quickly as possible, and I restructured my classes so that I could always turn on a short video or have them discuss something when I suddenly had to run out for a minute. I got so tired of calling attention to myself in meetings by so often having to get up and leave that I started just standing by the door so my constant (sometimes every two or three minutes) exits and reentries weren't as disruptive.

"Are you all right?" people asked. "You're running out to the bathroom an awful lot."

"Yeah, sorry about that," I said at first, but that response seemed dismissive, so after a while, I just started telling the matter-of-fact truth to whomever asked (well, except for my students): "I've been getting this bovine tuberculosis bacteria squirted into my bladder through tubes that get shoved up my penis, and the doctor says it's working, but it's wrecked the inside of my bladder and caused all kinds of random spasms that are making me virtually incontinent, so right now, I have to run out and pee sometimes every two or three minutes and that's just for now, by tomorrow, who knows, I might be wearing Depends." Now there's a way to get people to stop asking questions!

Before I had cancer, I had never understood why people on Facebook thought anyone would care that they'd "just eaten corn flakes for breakfast for the third day in a row!" or "hated that dress that Kim Kardashian is wearing on ET right now." Once my various symptoms, treatments, and related indignities became part of my new normal, though, everything was different. It's a slippery slope, I realized, from that kind of inane online sharing to the breaking down of any kind of barrier between what's in your head and what's in the public domain. The dictum "some things are better left unsaid" suddenly seemed as quaint and outdated as the post COVID-19 view of the days when people went to crowded bars and ate snacks out of community bowls.

After two years of scopes, scrapes, BCG treatments, trying to live a normal life before the next recurrence, and then repeating the process, my cancer came back yet again, this time in a more advanced stage, this time in the muscle itself, at which point I met with the Bladder King at Johns Hopkins Hospital. You can only imagine my surprise when instead of recommending the Whopper With Cheese Meal, he recommended removing my bladder entirely. The standard procedure was to replace it with an external bag, but since I was relatively young and (otherwise) relatively healthy, he suggested Plan-B, a much newer procedure, in which my bladder would be replaced with a piece of my intestine. They'd sew one end to my ureter and the other to my urethra, and *uroila!* It would work just like my old bladder.

What's not to like, I thought. *What could possibly go wrong,* I thought, shuddering at the possibilities.

The plan going in (and I mean that literally as well as metaphorically) was that they'd cut me open, take out my bladder, and do quickie biopsies of the surrounding lymph nodes, etc. If everything looked clean, they'd cut a section out of my intestine, build me a new bladder, reconnect everything, sew me up, and staple me shut. If they did see any complicating factors once they got in, they'd go back to Plan-A and give me an external bag. While I didn't relish the thought of wearing a bag for the rest of my life, the alternative seemed to be not having a life at all, so I acquiesced.

But before the surgery there was paperwork. My bladder cancer was my first serious encounter with the American healthcare bureaucracy that seems to be about protecting itself against lawsuits and lack of payment as much as (or more so than) about providing medical care. Here's an example:

This consent provides us with your permission to perform reasonable and necessary medical examinations, testing and treatment. By signing below, you are indicating that (1) you intend that this consent is continuing in nature even after a specific diagnosis has been made and treatment recommended; and (2) you consent to treatment at this office or any other satellite office under common ownership. The consent will remain fully effective until it is revoked in writing. You have the right at any time to discontinue services.

Who knew that an unintended consequence of bladder cancer treatment would be carpal tunnel syndrome from signing so many mind-numbing forms!

In addition to the liability forms, there were also forms that allowed them to share information about my condition. Ironically, at the same time my own personal disclosure barriers were breaking down, the institutional barriers were increasing. HIPAA, the Health Insurance Portability and Accountability Act, is the federal law that protects patients' rights, including their privacy, to the point where nobody's allowed to tell nobody nothin', at least not without all kinds of signed waiver forms.

So, at the same time I was happily telling anyone who'd listen about peeing out gigantic blood clots and being virtually incontinent and having tubes shoved up my penis, the surgeon and other hospital personnel weren't allowed to tell my wife and children whether I was alive or dead unless I'd signed countless waivers.

The surgery did, in fact, go according to plan. It lasted four-and-a-half hours, all of which I slept through, fortunately, and required four units of blood. They found nothing unexpected, built me a new bladder, and sent me on my way. "Sent me on my way" came after a week in the hospital, three weeks with a catheter, and the warning that I could never scuba dive.

They estimated that it would take me about six weeks to recover, not counting the subsequent incontinence, which they said might last a year or more before my muscles and nerves learned how to control this new chunk of plumbing. It's similar, apparently, to the way a stroke victim has to relearn how to control a part of their body that used to control itself automatically.

OK, so let's talk incontinence. I was somewhat leaky once the catheter came out, but within a short time was no longer peeing randomly all over the house, and within a couple weeks after that, my wife had me almost completely paper-trained. Within another couple weeks, I'd graduated (at least during the day) from Depends to big boy pants.

Once I was mobile and driving and my incision was healing reasonably well, it was time for physical therapy, two kinds of physical therapy. The first, as you might expect, was the kind that helps you rebuild your stamina and muscles after not doing anything for several weeks. The other was specifically about pelvic floor rehab to work on muscle and sphincter control to regain continence. Here's an example of the Pee-T's instructions to me:

Try to "squeeze" or contract your rectum as though you are trying not to "pass gas" in a public place. While "holding" this contraction, try to imagine you are "raising" or "lifting" your scrotum and testicles. Continue this contraction for a count of 10 seconds, then release and rest your entire pelvic floor for 10 seconds. Do this for 10 repetitions.

I imagined sitting at the family dinner table as a child and watching my parents' horrified expressions as our dinner guest said things like "rectum," "pass gas," "raising or lifting one's scrotum and testicles." And yet here I am, years later, putting all this out there for my children and grandchildren and old girlfriends to read.

My new bladder works really well, don't get me wrong, but not perfectly. Miraculously, that piece of intestine, once it became my bladder, started acting like a bladder. It learned to expand and contract, for example. But hard as it tried, it couldn't completely stop being intestine. For example, intestines are lined with mucous membrane, just like noses and mouths and throats. So, when I first started using it, the first thing I peed out was a little mucous plug that had collected. I still do sometimes, especially if I haven't peed for a while, but it's no big deal, except occasionally when I have to pee into a cup for my annual physical, and I hand it to the lab tech, and she looks at it and says, "Sir, do you know there's mucous in your urine?" and I say, "No, but if you hum a few bars, maybe—" at which point she cocks her head, dog-like, and walks away.

Another difference between a natural bladder and my intestinal bladder is that natural bladder tissue has nerves in it, so, for example, you know when you have to go. Intestinal tissue doesn't have nerves (who knew!), so I need to rely on one of three methods to tell me it's time to pee:

First: the clock. I try to pee every four hours or so, even though I don't feel the need to.

Second: various abdominal organs. If I wait too long, my bladder inflates and starts pushing against something or other that in turn, gives me a stomach ache or whatever kind of ache it might be. It made me more sympathetic toward pregnant women.

Third: leaking. You know how when you really have to go, you squeeze that little sphincter that keeps the urine from squirting out of your bladder and through your urethra? Or—if you're a boy—you squeeze that little sphincter in your penis that keeps you from wetting your pants and those around you? Men usually have three safety valves, so to speak, between them and incontinence: those two sphincters and also the prostate that pushes against the urethra and helps control the flow of urine. My new bladder, god love it, didn't come with a sphincter. And when they took out my bladder, they also took out my prostate. ("Oh, did we forget to tell you we were going to do that? Sorry.") The result is that instead of three safety valves between me and incontinence, I now only have one. And on rare occasions, especially at night when I'm not paying attention and my muscles are relaxed, not even that one works 100-percent.

Back when I was studying media effects research, I read a lot of scholarly articles that concluded that people who watched a lot of TV violence or consumed a lot of pornography or listened to a lot of profanity were less offended or otherwise affected by those behaviors than people who didn't experience that volume of those observed behaviors. Repeated exposure tended to break down long-held beliefs, attitudes, and social barriers. In my case, it wasn't violence or porn. It was two things: adapting to living in the new culture of American medicine that treats bodies clinically rather than personally; and then blurring the lines between living in that world and my "normal" world where certain boundaries still existed between what information and what level of detail we shared with "the public" and what we didn't.

Between the cystoscopes (the device through which they look at the inside of your bladder, scrape out cancer cells, and apply chemicals and other medications) and the catheters, I figure I've had tubes shoved up my penis 35 or so times.

And erectile dysfunction? Don't get me started!

My Name Was Jason

by Jonathan Aibel

On the south shore, an overdose claims a life every eight days
—Massachusetts Department of Public Health, 2014

> My palms so pale, palm to palm
> to hide the tremble of veins
> so blue with want.
>
> A little maple behind my bench
> holds leaves out to the sun
> touched with red
>
> where a single cricket insatiable
> chirps its goddamned brains
> out. I dream
>
> of drowning, of women who smell of dog:
> a few milliliters measure
> between light
>
> and darksome shit I am desperate to ditch,
> the endless tolling of funerals,
> fathers, uncles,
>
> lost to vikes or oxy taking
> a pain away, construction
> site contusions,

fatal accidents; news reporters
somber as if the end
of days, I live

this, this time, this need, this hunger.
When I open the door,
my red pit terrier

races, his mouth stupid-happy,
the baby smiles. This park
so sweet, and quiet.

The want is a wound September sun
can't warm, so deep, so who
is to say how to choose?

I bring my rig with me every day.

Fleeting Fossils

by Pamela Petro

During a chilly autumn, photographic images appeared on the sidewalks of Northampton, Massachusetts. The artist conjured art from concrete. But what did it mean and why do it? Read on...

Aisha's Image shortly after it was printed. Aisha was in the Fourth Grade when she took this picture

FLEETING FOSSILS

BY PAMELA PETRO

"Here, take it." A businessman, well dressed, briefcase under his arm. Offering me a dollar.
I laugh. I can't think of any other way to respond.
"Go on! It's for you." Impatience in his voice now.
"OK...thanks," I say uncertainly, assuming it's his way of supporting the arts.
After he strides away my student assistant, Suzanne, grabs my arm. "You realize," she says, tugging on my sleeve, "that he thought you were homeless, right?"
I look from my torn jeans and stained lumberjack shirt to the refrigerator-sized box next to us, wrapped in black plastic trash bags bound together with duct tape.
Of course. He thinks I live in our portable darkroom.
Too often, I feel I do.

During a chilly autumn in the late 2000's, Suzanne and I printed a series of 25 silver gelatin photographs, each about two feet by a foot and a half, on the sidewalks of Northampton, Massachusetts. I write this today and think, *Why on earth would anyone do that?*

The answer is pretty simple: it seemed like a good idea on paper. When I proposed it to the Black Rock Arts Foundation--which eventually gave me a grant to make the prints--I didn't know that concrete is a deviously fickle canvas. I didn't know how cold it got after dark in November, or how much that cold could slow down the developing time of black and white photos. I didn't know the Northampton DPW had a deep and grouchy regard for its sidewalks, because of which, after a week's time, I had to scrub the remains of each image off ice-cold concrete with a steel brush, knuckles bleeding, telling inquisitive passersby, "It's OK, I'm enacting a penance," so they'd leave me alone. (They did.)

Jon B's Image several days after printing

Above all, I didn't know how I'd feel wearing a headlamp jury-rigged with a red darkroom safelight, respirator covering mouth and nose, gloves turning hands to paws, on my hands and knees on the sidewalk, waiting in the dark--and waiting, waiting, waiting--for chemical magic to turn back time, to rekindle a moment of the near-past in silver and ash tones that would float up out of the pale concrete. I didn't know that relief and astonishment and elation could infuse my body with electric happiness when those tones came together in an image, or how the breath felt crushed from my lungs when they didn't.

It's good that I didn't know any of these things. Ignorance--and the frantic, problem-solving frenzy that bloomed in its path--made space for the sidewalk prints to be born.

uzanne and I weren't
rinting just any images on
dewalks. We were printing
fleeting fossils"--my name
or snapshots taken by
ourth graders at a local
chool and senior citizens
t a retirement community.
d given both groups single-
se cameras and asked them
o record their lives.
    Their photos included:
riends, parents, children,
rothers, sisters, the Red
ox, Spider Man, cats, dogs,
abbits, a gerbil, local
torefronts, flowers, family
arms, and one waffle iron.
    Once printed and exposed
o foot traffic and the
lements, their images--
ather like the fleeting
erspectives of children and
he elderly--didn't last long
efore they disappeared
ntirely. During their short
indow of visibility, they
terally lay underfoot as
he town went about its
usy-ness. Locals and
isitors, mostly in midlife,
eel-and-toe'd right over
hem as they talked and
lanned and stared ahead.

Alex's Image, immediately after printing

Nancy's Image, immediately after printing

I often spied on the
photos days after I'd printed
them, wondering how
people would react. Most of
the time passersby simply
didn't notice the large-
format, original prints
they were walking across.
Occasionally someone
stopped and took a photo
of the photo. But most
of the time the big
images were just as over-
looked as the perspectives
of the photographers who
took them.

We had a system. On the
afternoon of a printing
session I'd go downtown
and paint large rectangles
on the sidewalk with white-
wash. Then I'd mumble a
few pleas to the universe.
    Suzanne and I would
meet at dusk. A friend had
framed a refrigerator-
sized box for us out of
2 x 4s, adding a removeable
top: this was the portable
darkroom the businessman
thought I lived in, around
which we'd wrapped black
felt and plastic. We'd set

*Left, Nancy's Image--as soon as I moved the portable darkroom away a cyclist rode right over the print.
Right: image by one of the local schoolchildren*

the box over a painted rectangle and then one of us would slip on the darkroom headlamp and crawl underneath. Our task: paint liquid photo emulsion onto the white space and dry it with a hairdryer, powered by a portable generator borrowed from a local motorcycle shop.

A tricky moment next: using an old-fashioned slide projector turned on its side, we'd beam a negative directly onto the sidewalk through a small hole in the top of the "contraption," as we'd taken to calling the portable darkroom.

Then we'd sneak looks at each other to gauge which of us had more nerve at that very moment. The evening's designated magician would then crawl back under the contraption, headlamp and respirator strapped in place and bearing two spray bottles, one of developer solution, the other of fix. Our goal: coax the image to reluctant life.

Developing was easy; fixing was terrifying. When had the image developed enough? When had it gone too far? The process was unforgiving. Often we either over or under exposed the prints.

Marcus' Image the morning after it was printed and the emulsion had frozen and cracked

Sometimes the sidewalk texture proved too rough to yield a clear picture. (I soon became a connoisseur of concrete.) We learned early--but wrenchingly--to never again print on a street-corner: headlights of cars making lefthand turns swept like avenging lighthouse beams beneath the darkroom's skirts and blackened our prints, no matter what precautions we took.

Heartbreak lurked in the mornings, too. The emulsion of meticulously printed images some-times froze overnight and cracked as it warmed the next day, shattering into a hundred jigsaw pieces. (And this is why we as a people don't print on sidewalks.) But rain proved our greatest enemy.

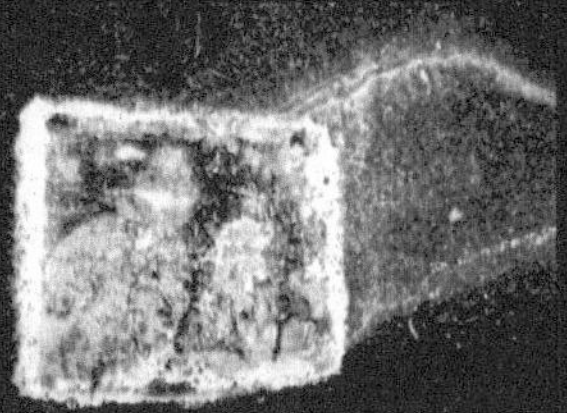

In the end none of this mattered. Not our fierce brainstorming nor the quality of the images; not the fact that I was able to successfully scrub the sidewalks clean for the DPW. From con-ception to documentation, focusing on the prints themselves put us in danger of missing the point. As the fall wore on we came to realize--it caught us by surprise--that "Fleeting Fossils" was always, from start to finish, a performative work. It was the process that mattered, not the results.

Suzanne and I gradually attracted an amorphous, nighttime following of college students and homeless people. They helped us carry the generator, the contraption, our buckets and hair dryer and slide projector. We provided strange and unlooked-for entertainment, purpose, and community, and left souvenirs on the sidewalks to prove, by light of morning, that together we'd conjured art from concrete the night before.

We also made a few historic prints from c. 1900, courtesy of Historic Northampton Museum.

Will Work for Textbooks

by Michelle Gurule

Jack was breaking the rules of our arrangement the first time he told me he loved me. I was twenty-four years old, and I was his sugar baby. The guidelines we'd agreed on had come nine months earlier via an iMessage that Jack had typed completely in Baby Boomer innuendos: *I would like to get to first base, second base and third base, but the more often we do homeruns, the more gifts you will get.* ☺

Gifts was 'sugar lingo' for things like shoes and jewelry. I learned this from the internet after I'd met Jack at a club, where he'd slipped me four-hundred-dollars, his business card and a proposition to have dinner with him. Paid, cash. I googled *sugar baby,* only to find that the most respectable literature about this kind of arrangement was tucked away in a Reddit thread: *New to the sugar bowl, what do I need to know?* This prompted me to search the term 'sugar bowl' which at first only pulled up a lot of dessert recipes, but, as it turned out, the sugar bowl was a term that embodied the whole world of sugaring, sort of like the wizardly world of Harry Potter.

Gingerbaby96 posted: *Sex is required*, and *The price will be decided by you and your sugar daddy (often abbreviated as SD)*.

Newbabe wrote: *The sex could be good or bad, depending on how eager your SD is to please you.*

Sugarsugar knew a lot about the financial aspect. She said: *Start buying things with cash, don't put your money in a bank, and if you must, never, ever make a transaction more than $10,000 or the bank must report it to the IRS.*

Jack's love declaration came about in the fall semester of my final year of college.

The FAFSA awards had just been offered, and I logged into my university account, hitting "decline" for the first time in my life. My college journey had been long and inconsistent: two-time drop out and twice returned.

All prior semesters had been paid for via a blend of subsidized and unsubsidized loans. Had I logged into my Sallie Mae account, I would've seen an ever-expanding figure reaching upwards of $35,000. Bold and awaiting payback. With 'moderate' interest rates between 4-7%.

I'd paid for the semester's tuition out of my own pocket, with money I'd earned from giving blow jobs to Jack.

I clicked the mousepad with all the might my finger possessed—it was a click stronger than all the accumulated *Accept* clicks of the past. *Good for me*, I thought, for being so responsible with my money.

It was bigger than the fact I'd saved and allocated $3,656 for my education, but I understood that I'd just dodged a decade of accumulated interest on a loan I no longer had to take out. Had there been a bottle of champagne nearby, I would've popped that baby open and chugged it straight from the lip.

"Whoopity-do," I cried out to my laptop screen. "Thank you, Jack!"

Wanting to share my accomplishment, I decided to ring my dad.

My father was my best friend. While we'd always been close growing up, his second divorce ran parallel to a recent break up of my own. We bonded over nightly phone calls where we'd recount our daily dramas. Sharing our pain made us feel less alone, less miserable, like it was almost funny.

I'd first told him about Jack while he and I were sitting in our local mall's food court. I was only one week into my sugaring arrangement. My dad and I shared a lemonade and a footlong corndog from Hot Dog on a Stick. My sister was there, too.

He asked me if there was a difference between sugar babying and prostitution. "Sort of," I explained. Sure, I was being paid for sex, but with sugar babying there were specific rules that Jack and I had agreed upon. I was making $1,200 a week, to spend one hour with Jack in La Quinta Inns. According to a 2018 stat from *seeking-arrangement.net*, that was nearly double the national average, which the site claimed had been $2,800 a month per baby.

"Well, Shell," he slurped the straw. "It's not great, but as long as no one's getting hurt. Who am I to judge?"

I nodded in agreement. My whole family seemed to agree that the arrangement was a lifeboat—come to save me from the sinking ship of my broke ass life—but what I didn't know then was that after the sessions, when Jack would clean himself in the shower, I'd be putting my head in my hands and repeating to myself: *I can't do this. I can't do this.* I would never tell anyone the dark turn it would take, not wanting my family to know that I thought I might be getting hurt. Not in the physical way, but the invisible kind of damage. The kind that would make me wonder if I had gone bankrupt inside. The kind that would make me question what kind of person I was.

In the weeks between that conversation at the mall and declining the loans, when I left the hotel rooms with Jack—when I would feel sorry for myself—I'd think about my dad and the labor of his own body. How as a child he'd spent several months out of every school year living on migrant farms in Idaho, harvesting potatoes with his family. Sugaring—the tasks of the job—were hard on me in one way, sure, but so easy in another. Wasn't I lucky? I would ask myself, as I counted out the money: always given to me in white bank envelopes after the fact. Stacks of hundred-dollar bills. *Yes,* I'd think. *Just like I'd won the lottery.*

But when I called him, he wasn't impressed.

"You just lost yourself a vacation to Mahi-Mahi," he said.

"Isn't Mahi-Mahi a fish?" I asked.

My dad assured me that the location wasn't the important forfeiture here, but the trip.

"You should be using the money to live your life, Shell. You think for a second student loans are going to matter in the apocalypse?" He quickly pivoted the conversation into something he found much more interesting: a survival lesson. "You want to make a good investment?" he asked me. "Buy a gun."

Given that my father was convinced the world was on the verge of total collapse, his advice scattered between clinically insane and financially astute. And while my mother was more well-rounded in some areas, she was drowning in debt accrued mostly from charging too many hamburgers and sweet teas from McDonalds. My father had found her credit card statements and asked how it was possible for someone to owe so much without anything aside from a few spare pounds to show for it. The answer was simple: consistency and only making minimum payments for over a decade.

"I think it was a good investment," I said. Aside from sharing my student loan joy, there was one other matter I needed advice on. Jack had recently offered me a 'gift': buying my school books for the semester. "What do you think I should do?" I asked my dad.

"You know what I think," he said. "Take it. Cha-ching!"

A few weeks earlier, after declining another one of Jack's gift offers—a new iPhone—my father talked me off what he referred to as a "stupidity cliff." This time we were eating lunch inside Taco Bell's "cantina."

I'd always prided myself on saying no to Jack's gift offers, thinking it was the most responsible thing to do. In terms of sugar daddies, he was already being pretty generous, paying me over a grand a week for an hour of my time and moderate access to my body. Back when Jack had first made the arrangement offer, penetration had been agreed upon, but as it would turn out, Jack would lose his erection whenever the condom came out. While my duties decreased from sex to blow jobs, the original figure still stood. This made me feel like I'd gotten a pretty stupendous deal.

So why take Jack up on gifts when I didn't actually need them? What I wanted was to get out of debt so I could get my real life started. Had he proposed making student loan payments for me, I would've said HELL YES, and even provided him the login credentials, entrusting him with my social security number and address— so he could make payments from the comfort of his own home.

"Anything, and I mean *anything* Jack offers you, you should take," my dad told me. He saw this simply as good business. To him, any gift was just the opportunity to own something nice.

I wanted to tell my dad that it was complicated to receive. I worried if I took Jack up on these little side offers, he would think I was getting too much for what I was giving him. I didn't want to encourage Jack to look for a sugar baby that required less. Like, unprotected sex. *Seekingarrangement.net* advertises to men on their homepage, "Four babies per sugar daddy—the odds are in your favor!" I needed to be as low-maintenance as possible; I thought of this as job security.

I spared my dad the details and just said, "I don't think that's a good idea. He's not even offering me things that I want."

"Oh my god," my dad said. He was using a plastic spork to scrape clean the boat his Nacho Supreme had been served in—no bean or chip crumb that he'd paid for would be wasted. "I thought I raised you better than that." My father shook his head at me, truly disappointed, and then lifted his spork to his lips. What went into his mouth appeared to be a full tablespoon of sour cream. "Next time he offers you something you don't want, you say, 'Yes, thank you, Jack,' and then you give it to one of us."

"You don't even know what an iPhone is," I said.

"Nope, but I know what free is."

This is essentially where my dad, and my larger family, got things wrong with Jack. At the time, I was living with my mom in a compact two-bedroom apartment in Aurora, a suburb outside of Denver. My sister and my seven-year-old nephew also lived there. Our number one rule to a cohesive environment was a complete lack of boundaries, seeing as it would've been impossible to respect any of them anyway. Given that I disappeared for one hour a week, only to return home with an envelope of cash, and, often times, bags of takeout, they had all started to see *sugar daddy* as a synonym for *magic genie*. A mythical creature on whose chubby little belly I simply had to rub my palm around, as I made countless wishes, and then PLOP! He would shit out iPhones and chocolate lava cakes and stacks of hundred-dollar bills. But this was what being poor was like: wealth to my mom and dad was as foreign and enticing as a genie. And the sudden wealth I had just seemingly stumbled into was as mystifying as a magic wish: appearing, it seemed, out of thin air.

I did not ask my family to think of what these gifts cost me, and so they viewed sugaring through the lens of money and things like food, dental work, my mom's overdue hospital bills, and paying for college semesters out of pocket—all the things that made sex work seem like a really good opportunity for me, for all of us. I understood how the iPhone seemed to my father like the prize of some raffle ticket giveaway. I saw how he could think I was being silly by not saying yes to everything I was offered.

Even though I knew everything sugar daddies gave came at a cost, the conversation with my dad inspired me to take Jack up on his 'gift.' I texted him after hanging up the phone to my dad: *Hello! ↜ Hope you're having a wonderful day! Can't wait to see you tomorrow! Do you remember when you told me you'd buy my school books? I'm buying them all today, and I was just wondering if the offer still stands* ☺

His response was quick. It almost always was: *Yes! I'll reimburse you for them. Just let me know the price* ☺ *You're so smart and sexy. I like to make your life easy.*

I opted to buy all of my books off used websites, so my semester total came to a mere $200, but I looked on Amazon for the prices I'd give Jack. "Come on, baby," I said to my laptop. "I want full price items and I want those shipping and handling costs." A fiction anthology I bought was a lousy $.01 cents on *Valore.com* but could also be purchased brand new for $45. After shipping, that would be $41 dollars for me.

The total of all my books, plus $100 for the hassle of my research, came to $493.

I texted Jack the number and he promised he wouldn't forget to bring it the next night to our weekly pleasure session. It really was that easy. He was always that easy.

"Like stealing candy from a daddy," I said, feeling like I had gotten away with something.

When I pulled up to the motel the following evening, Jack was already in the parking lot, leaning against the trunk of his shiny BMW.

As usual, Jack was wearing a white polo and khaki pants. Such a common outfit for him that it took on the effect of a uniform. He was so consistent. Unabashedly his same old self every time. I would have found Jack boring if I loved him, but as a sugar baby there was so much safety in his lack of change. There was no surprise. No mystery. I was grateful for that.

Once inside the room, we sat on the bed side by side, the lengths of our outer thighs pressed into one another. We shared a complimentary package of cookies the motel chain left inside the rooms. This night it was peanut butter.

Jack had requested that at the start of every pleasure session we 'share' at least five minutes of conversation. On a few occasions, not knowing what else to say, Jack had asked me, "So, um, what kind of vegetables do you like?" I quickly learned to take the reins.

"How was your day?" I asked him.

Jack's face was long, tired. The bags under his eyes were puffy. I listened to him gripe about his boss. Something about the task being too large, the timeframe being too short, and therefore impossible.

I nodded my head, agreeing with him. "That sounds so unfair," I said. "You work so hard, you deserve to feel appreciated." I chose my words wisely. These were the right things to say. I'd learned this from the Reddit thread, too. I was there to listen. Never to offer suggestions. Never to engage in a real conversation. Just to let him unload.

"Thank you, sweetie," he said. "You're so nice to me."

He really meant it.

It was in moments like this one that Jack's loneliness radiated off of him like something toxic. As I ran my hand up along his back and tickled him with my fingers, I understood that he was paying me as much to sit next to him and ask about his day and rub his neck, as he was for the sex stuff. That's how I tried to convince myself that, of the two of us, I was getting the better end of the deal.

Sure, Jack had cash and I needed it, but money was not exclusive to him. If I wanted to quit sugaring, I could go elsewhere and work and make money. Granted, I would earn substantially less, but it would be no different than the currency he slid into those bank envelopes. A dollar I earned from sugar babying was no more valuable than a dollar I could've earned working at a grocery store.

The things I gave Jack—what any sugar baby could've given him—were different, in as much that they were not genuine. What Jack wanted on an emotional level—to be desired, to be listened to, to be cared for—were not things one could simply buy. I was easily replaceable, I knew this, but no matter what woman Jack hired to touch him, the desire he would purchase from her would be counterfeit. The intimacy at the other end of a dollar dissipated the moment the motel doors shut behind him.

Sometimes I felt bad for him.

Twenty-five minutes later—while I was giving him a blow job—Jack said, "I love you."

Jack had never tried to push the rules before. Surely, I thought, I had heard him wrong. But, then he said it again: "I love you, Michelley. I really love you."

My whole body went cold as I looped the question: *how could Jack possibly think he loved me?* He did not really know me. How much can be known in a just few minutes of obligatory conversation? This brought about a new anxiety: if Jack didn't really know me, then I didn't really know him. Time slowed to a crawl. My skin tingled as my capillaries expanded to their maximum width. I was a sex worker in a motel, which matched the victim profiles of about 110% of the *Law and Order SVU* episodes I'd seen. What if Jack was one of those men, who, after he'd decided he loved me, wanted me to love him back, and when that didn't happen, and it would never happen, he would kill me, and skin me and turn me into a lamp? My circulatory system sent a message to my brain, through a 1/3 blood, 2/3 adrenaline cocktail: *You have gotten yourself into real a mess.*

I handled the situation by ignoring it. I had to hold on to the faith that Jack's uttering of the words "I love you" was more so for himself than to be shared with me. Maybe words of affirmation outbursts were a symptom of his chronic loneliness. Maybe he just wanted to hear it out loud. And yet: I was frightened. My body, all at once, felt valuable and valueless.

In a better world, I could pretend the rules of the arrangement were always ours. That Jack and I had met in those rooms each week with our expectations at eye level, which was how sugar babying was supposed to work. But, in the real world, Jack had the money, and therefore it was he who called the shots.

Maybe it seems insignificant, but I was already giving Jack my body, something I deemed separate from my *true* essence. In order to survive selling sex, I prided myself on my ability to keep the real me—the one that I was convinced really mattered—out of the deal. My body was one thing and it sat inside a box, but, to me, love was much bigger, and encompassed the whole world outside of that box. I didn't want Jack to have it, nor did I want him to think he could buy it.

If I had been braver; if I had seen myself as Jack's equal and not at his disposal, I think I would've stopped him. I think I would've ruined the pleasure session. I think I would've killed the mood, because then I wouldn't have been afraid of what sat on the other side of my speaking up.

I often think about the cultural image of good sex workers and how they stay empowered. Think Julia Roberts and her mantra in *Pretty Woman*: "We say who, we say when, we say how much." But this is where any power I want to believe I had slips away from me: I could not stand up to Jack—to say that I had not agreed to using the words "I love you"—without losing my job. If I did not play along with Jack's rules then he could find someone else who would. *Jack says who, Jack says what, Jack says how much.* The odds were in his favor.

The truth, when I write it, does not feel empowering. I was a pawn.

As the minutes passed inside the motel room, Jack moaned into the air, and the fear that had pooled into my belly hardened into a concrete fist. I felt dirty in a brand-new way. I wondered if I had inadvertently given Jack permission to take more by accepting the textbooks. I was a sugar baby after all. Nothing he gave me ever came from the kindness of his heart, no matter how much either of us wanted to pretend it was so.

I worked hard to make the blow job end faster, and when Jack came into a stiff bleached washcloth, he did so with one final, "I love you!" It sounded like a sneeze. I sat up my on my knees, relieved that I was nearly free to go to my car and leave the night behind. My heart beat pulsed inside my ears as I looked down at Jack's face. His head was pressed into the pillow. His eyes were shut. A grin crept across his lips. Jack was pleased with himself. Happy. In love?

When I spoke to my dad later that night, I told him Jack paid for the textbooks, that I had finally "accepted a gift."

"Good job, Shell," he said.

Good job. I had done right.

"Hopefully in the spring he offers to pay for the whole semester."

Just imagine, I thought. *He'd end up calling me his wife.*

Remembrance Day
by Daniel E. Pritchard

for John W. Pritchard, Jr.

We should remember
all the dead of
the Sixth Marines.

They who survived
the Battle of Okinawa,
its rot stench under

a "typhoon of steel,"
then they prepared to die
on a beach in Kyushu.

Instead, I am focused on
the hush of sliding doors
and a pair of bare elms,

two laced plumes
rising over the snow
in the flat cold,

their tangled branches
like bronchioles, vivisected,
exhausting the light.

I am exhausted.
Inside the hospital,
my grandfather lies

pale on white sheets,
his body held in
a position of least pain.

His hatchling mouth
pops open. He pecks
at the stale, dry air.

Because we were not
in the sixth Marines,
mom and I have trouble

with words. Dying, dead.
We avoid them by ironing,
bickering, washing sheets.

Because every word,
given the time, eventually
rhymes with silence,

Pa was a poet of silences.
Of course we asked
about the war—

mom begged him once
to explain what it meant
to be a China Marine.

DANIEL E. PRITCHARD

Pa looked at his shoes
and said *Well, I guess*
we were Marines

and we were in China.
Not long after that,
he and I were down in

the basement workshop
puzzling some little repair.
He asked for the measure.

I handed it to him.
The rain had started
to leak into the sump.

It kicked on behind us,
purring rhythmically.
I hadn't said a word.

The war, he said,
wasn't how you imagine.
We laid in open graves.

We fired into the dark.
You couldn't see
so you shot at nothing.

We hated the darkness
but we hated the light too.
Flares and fire. A plane

came down no more
than fifty yards away
from my position, sent up

a column of smoke
like we were in the Bible
wandering the desert.

We dug foxholes with short-
handled spades and waited.
The kid next to me got hit

over his left eye. Eighteen,
from West Virginia.
He died before his hands

could drop his rifle.
He'd never worn shoes
until boot camp. He died.

And that's it. That's all.
I didn't die. So many
guys died, but I didn't.

He stopped to clean his
glasses with the undershirt
he used for a rag, then

Pa laid the square and drew
a line across the board.
He measured the cut then

pulled the saw across
the grain in long, solid strokes.
I could hear the pant of pine

giving way beneath that saw
in the sterile untidiness
of Pa's hospital room,

the wet breath collapsing
in his brittle chest,
the ward doors

opening and closing
in the bright cold sun.
He struggled to hold

a cup of water. He tore
the IVs out of his arms.
He refused to eat. He lay

half-naked on the bed with
swollen joints and sores,
wires and tubes branching

out of the riveted hull
of his history, rocking,
unevenly rocking and

his heart expectant still
as in the moment before
they'd all come ashore.

We should remember
all the dead
of the Sixth Marines.

We may never see their
like again; may we
never see their like again.

Architectures of New England
by Daniel E. Pritchard

I.

The ocean's adulation of the shore
is not a Sunday miracle. Its waves evangelize

the heathered seawall. They canonize
the lacework grass. Shingled roofs rise up

to rhyme with peaking breakers.
Its empire is the mind. Thus our sense

of what perfection is the sea:
the one and one of interlocking chimes,
the zero of its lunacy.

Marbled skies hold the cycle of its *Ave*
in our chapped lips. The waters
border nothing, having swallowed leviathan.

II.

Glazed with frost, pine trees shush
the stuttering clapboard. Weathervanes

trace Virgo and the hunter's cross.
Saints' dark eyes in the hammerbeam
stare blank into blank. Days collapse

like cellophane in fire—a helix
and a nocturne. Confession turns up
unexpected as a missing key.
The chancel drowns my knee.

The blue rose window dilates with frost.
Psalms fill the time. Steps fill the time.

Prayer promises clarity. Prayer promises
clarity and I repeat myself. Like my father.
I repeat myself as the bells of vigil wake.

III.

Does everything make a church?

Even the evening sky
is column and crest, a violet nave

that echoes in the fifty-story glass

while low-rise worker boxes
weep their leaded paint.

Monotone seabirds
pebble the shore.

Estuarial itself, time.
Each next surge transmutes the last

like the tongues of pine that lay a floor.

Why does everything make a church?

The one and one of interlocking chimes.
Like my father, I repeat myself.

Pandemic Story Problems

by Naomi J. Williams

1. Mariah gets a temporary job that pays her $1 on Day One. On the second day, her pay is doubled to 2 dollars. Her daily wage doubles every day thereafter, for 30 days. How much money does she make on the 30th day? How much has she earned in one month?

2. Same question, only change "gets a temporary job that pays her $1" to "contracts a virus." Change "her pay is doubled" to "she transmits the virus" and "dollars" to "people." Then change "Her daily wage" to "The number of new infections," etc. You get the picture. The new questions are: Assuming an unlimited number of available people, how many new infections occur on that 30th day? And how many total have been infected in one month?

3. Congratulations. You've learned about exponential growth! Fix yourself a gin and tonic: one part gin to two parts tonic, poured over ice, finished with a squeeze of lime. You only have half an ounce of gin left? Sad! Well, how much tonic, expressed as a fraction of a cup, can you add to your half-ounce

of gin and maintain the 1:2 ratio? (It's just as well, you know. You have so many problems left to go. You need to stay alert!)

4. Tan is a multimedia artist and part-time dog-walker. Assuming he walks three dogs a day, five days a week, for $20 per walk, and takes four weeks off per year, how much does he gross in a year? Now assume his clients tip him an average of 15% (some tip more; really rich people tend to tip less, of course). How much does he gross then?

5. When the epidemic arrives, all of Tan's dog-walking clients cancel. What percentage of his clients offer to continue to pay him?

   a. 0%
   b. 25%
   c. 50% (haha! as if)

6. But then—hallelujah—Tan's $1200 stimulus check arrives. After admiring the president's signature, he deposits his check (using on-line banking, of course; no dangerous trips to the ATM). Disregarding tips, how many days' worth of dog-walking does this check cover?

7. Tan lives in a tiny, not-at-all-up-to-code Brooklyn apartment with a mold problem; his rent is $1500/month. Tan hands over the entire $1200 from his stimulus check to the landlord, who says he will only allow Tan to remain in the apartment on a pro-rated basis. Assuming a 30-day month, how many days does Tan have left in the apartment?

8. Are you quibbling now about the real cost of housing in New York or how eviction proceedings actually work? Dude. It's a math problem. Go fix yourself another drink. But first make up your own problem that involves converting liquid measures from metric to American.

9. Tan's landlord contracts the dread virus and dies alone in his apartment. Math can be a bitch, but so can karma. Ponder for a while the incalculable mystery.

10. Tan calls up his friend Mariah. Mariah has this remarkable temp job where her daily wage doubles every day. "Can I get in on that?" Tan asks. "No," Mariah says. "I'm being made an example of." But, she says, she's buying a 14-unit apartment building in Midtown for $16 million so she and her family and friends can quarantine together, and she offers him a one-bedroom unit rent-free. Based on your calculations from Problem #1, and ignoring taxes and Mariah's other expenses, on which day will she have earned enough to buy the building outright?

11. Mariah's too-good-to-be-true temp job involves selling N95 masks to hospitals. Before the pandemic, the masks sold for $2 apiece. But now she's entertaining—and accepting—bids for as much as $1500 per case. If a case contains 20 boxes of 10 masks each, how much of a price-gouger is she?

12. Bonus True or False: At least Mariah and her company aren't as bad as the federal government, whose agents swoop in and commandeer the masks before they can be delivered to the hospitals that already paid for them.

13. The City will be on lockdown for 135 days, then re-opened slowly, slowly, slowly. Tan and Mariah emerge from their Midtown apartments blinking like optometry patients who've just had their eyes dilated. How long will it be before their lives feel normal again?

a. It can take four to six hours for eyes to return to normal after dilation.

b. A month or two.

c. Normal? What is wrong with you?

Mourning in the Time of COVID-19

by Angelique Tung

Tuesday, April 21st: "Mom's in the ER. Dr. recommends hospice," reads a text from my sister.

My mother's dementia is not new but this message from my sister brings an urgency to the situation. That night over family dinner of calamari pasta in red sauce, I discuss the possibility of visiting my mother in California. "If I go," I tell them, "I'll have to isolate for two weeks when I get back to Boston."

"We'll starve to death," my sixteen year old cries as he twirls linguine around his fork. The irony of my son's comment strikes me hard as my mother lay in a hospital bed 3,000 miles away unable to eat. Starving.

Can I live with myself if I don't visit my mother? Can I leave my family for more than two weeks during a pandemic? These questions loop in my head. I'm stuck like a blender without enough liquid. I call my sister who is sitting vigil at my mother's bedside. "This situation seems impossible right now. How do I choose?"

Despite my ambivalence, I search flights to California and evaluate my options given the new COVID-19 restrictions. I contemplate flying alone, across the country on an empty plane. Is my risk of getting COVID-19 greater at 30,000 feet or in the aisle of my local grocery store? My thoughts toggle between saying goodbye to my mother or continuing the humble task of feeding my family.

Wednesday, April 22nd: "Nursing director says a couple of weeks but if you look it up, if mom not able to drink fluids, then 4-5 days."

During the past several weeks of our isolation as my mother's health deteriorates and she loses her ability to walk, speak or eat, I occupy my time thinking about cooking food, compiling shopping lists, and planning meals. Feeding my family has been a comfort now more than ever. I assuage my fears by serving meals of flank steak with chimichurri sauce, salmon with tomato coulis, fresh blueberry muffins, and homemade chocolate cake topped with ganache frosting. If I feed them well, they won't notice we've been unable to leave the house for what feels like a million consecutive days. My focus on daily cooking confers normalcy in our otherwise mundane routine.

Though there aren't many, one of my favorite memories of my mother and me is in our tiny kitchen in my childhood home in Northern California. I sat on a yellow phone book at our oval Formica table hollowing out the doughy insides of an éclair so my mother could inject them with creamy vanilla custard. Once filled, she'd dribble streams of dark melted chocolate delicately over each one. My mouth watered as I admired the glossy desserts sitting side by side on the wire rack.

Thursday, April 23rd: "No IV in hospice, offer of fluids but late dementia patients not able to swallow."

During the cold winter months, my mother filled our pot-bellied stove with kindling to warm the kitchen in preparation of bread baking. She'd spend the morning making the dough starter by meticulously mixing packages of yeast with warm milk and sugar. Hours later after the yeast had proofed, she'd carefully measure out flour and massage the mixture to create mounds of dough that she'd divide and set into individual glass bowls, cover them with dishtowels and place near the stove where they'd rise overnight. By the time I woke up the next morning, she'd already started kneading the dough balls that had grown twice in size. I'd watch the muscles on her arms tighten as she punched, rolled and kneaded the dough into submission. Before the dough balls went into the baking pans, she'd fold in tomato sauce for a savory loaf or peanut butter or cinnamon for breakfast bread. She'd carefully place the buttered pans into the pre-heated oven. I'd sit on the floor and peer through the small window, the smell of baking bread intoxicating as I waited for the finished loaves so I could have a warm slice smothered in butter.

Friday, April 24th: "Mom's talking a bit. I just fed her yogurt since caregiver was serving dinner to others. She's drinking juice."

During the week, my mother made sandwiches for my school lunch. Pale, peach colored tomato bread sandwiches filled with fresh-caught albacore tuna, stood out like beacons beckoning my classmates to mock me. "What are you eating?" one student said. "It smells like tuna fish." Ewwww," others chimed in. What I'd do for fresh albacore on toasted slabs of my mother's tomato bread now.

I saw that bread baking was an arduous process and used that logic to convince my mother to buy Wonder Bread from Safeway. "Think of all the time you'll save." I'd follow her down the bread aisle and search for the red, blue and yellow packaging. I'd squeeze the soft loaves and was amazed how the bread retained my tiny handprint and wondered if an unsuspecting customer might notice? I didn't realize at the time that we were poor and that store-bought bread was more expensive than a packet of yeast. Still, I wanted to fit in and believed a Jif peanut butter sandwich and store-bought jam slathered between two pasty white tasteless slices of Wonder Bread would help make me popular or a the very least allow me to blend in.

Saturday, April 25th: "Sleeps a lot but then wakes up for short periods of time, eyes open, we offer juice or water."

On Sunday I plan our weekly menu: chicken tikka masala, scallops on fennel, and beef Bolognese. Sitting at my desktop computer I scroll through my favorite cooking blogs for new recipe ideas. I gaze at Instagram photos of steaming loaves of bread. I'm ashamed that despite my love of cooking and baking, I haven't found the courage to try this quarantine-inspired trend. I tried baking bread, pre-pandemic, and failed. My yeast had gone bad and my proof didn't materialize. Perhaps I'm lazy or maybe I know I'll never be able to recreate that memory of my mother, strong and active as she kneaded life-sustaining bread. I realize my family needs me to feed them now more than ever. That's what I choose to believe.

Sunday, April 26th: "Mom still able to take in water by sucking sponge. Hard for her to swallow."

The truth is, I don't want to fly to California to watch my mother choking on her own saliva. I can't bear to see her mouth frozen. I won't see my mother's once vibrant blue eyes dimmed. Would she recognize me? Would I be sad if she didn't? I decide to stay home and continue wearing the same pajama pants I've had on for the past seventeen days.

In the midst of my cooking and baking, I feel guilty knowing that my mother can no longer eat, chew or swallow. I recall our last meal together when I visited her in 2017. She asked me to meet her at Denny's, the restaurant equivalent of Wonder Bread. We didn't discuss her dementia as she devoured a stack of pancakes drowning in fake maple syrup. I dream that when the quarantine is over, I can visit my mother again. I will bake tomato bread and feed her a slice smothered with butter. Until then, I bake pumpkin muffins and make white bean soup with organic kale to sustain us.

On Thursday, April 30th at approximately 12:30 p.m. my mother passed. My sister calls me. "Hi baby," she says.

"Mom's gone?" I ask. I sit down on the gray sectional. My boys appear in the kitchen and come sit next to me. After I hang up, they hug me and tell me they love me. We hold each other. Their words are a counterbalance to the sadness I feel, a type of cardiac superglue mending my broken heart. Then, my sixteen year old asks, "Can you cut my hair now?" Life goes on. We order takeout. Maybe Indian from Singh's Café? I don't remember eating that night or the next.

In the days after she died, I convince myself I made the right choice. But today, as I stand at the kitchen sink washing Spanish rice and shrimp encrusted bowls, I question my decision. My decision came down to this: would I have gone if not for a deadly virus?

My husband comes downstairs and asks if I'm okay. He senses my mood and understands my uncertainty.

"You know, we would have survived without you." He's right but his words slice me. But, could I have survived without them? I know the answer.

Several months have passed, our lives a perpetual holding pattern. We can't plan a memorial service for my mother until COVID-19 is eradicated.

In the meantime, I pickle cucumbers and red onions, bake zucchini bread, and grill hand spun pizza on the barbecue. We devour plates of seafood chorizo paella, coconut cauliflower curry and penne alla vodka (extra vodka) topped with fresh basil from my garden. I still have not found the courage or the yeast to bake bread. For now, I will take time to mourn my mother. I will honor her by feeding my family as if my life depends on it.

To Silence

by José Angel Araguz

I never questioned
your meeting me here.
You've decided to hold

the place of my father,
no body, only
the air between us.
You slip behind
each word,

and crowd. Marching
beside my next breath,
which for you
is a kind of blank page,

I am learning
to get a sense
of where we're going.

Youth

by José Angel Araguz

Youth is a pig, a certain nervousness.

Blindly, youth trots in,
makes its noise.

Its comma-mouth keeps running on.

You grow comfortable with youth,
stay up each night.

At every turn: rain, music, whatever.

Only later do you feel
(eyes red

from every bristle
of coming light) how

the husky snout roots through your heart.

For Greenwood

by Celeste Cosme

When my husband and I were much younger and had more leisure time, we decided to binge-watch *Buffy the Vampire Slayer*. It was my husband's idea. I had watched the show when I was a teenager but didn't religiously tune in every week. About three episodes in, I realized this was not one of our best decisions. My husband is 6 feet tall, broad-shouldered, with arms the size of my abdomen, but he is a total wimp when it comes to scary shows and movies. In the middle of the night, I woke up to him walking around our tiny apartment with a novelty ninja sword, similar to the one each of his brothers owned. Something about a childhood love of anime. He claimed he heard something in the kitchen. I understood why he was frightened and we giggled ourselves into enough bravery to go back to bed and didn't click play on *Buffy* the next night.

When I met my husband, I was at a church in Tulsa, the one I'd joined soon after moving from New Jersey to Oklahoma. The church was called Greenwood Christian Center, and it was named after the street corner of Greenwood and Archer, the place where

"the single worst incident of racial violence in American history"
took place. When I was in high school, I'd never read about the
Tulsa Race Massacre, a term I much prefer to the "Race Riot" as
it is more often referred to. Over the course of two days, May 31
to June 1 of 1921, the white people of Tulsa terrorized 35 square
blocks known as Black Wall Street; another piece of history I'd nev-
er learned about. The Greenwood district of Tulsa was the wealthi-
est Black community in the United States at the time. Someone once
told me that money could change hands over and over again amid
Black society there without ever leaving Greenwood.

I have not watched the video of George Floyd's murder. I
don't know if I ever will. I have seen the still images and read the
transcript. For me, that is already too much. I understand that the
footage must be something wholly different from the other killings
caught on tape. Floyd's slaying has galvanized a nation and ener-
gized people of all races and ages to come together and protest na-
tionally and globally. Some people have supposed that the reason
the response to his death has been so much greater than after the
death of others before him is because he called out for his deceased
mother while dying; a fact that brings me to tears. I'm not sure I
need to see the video.

Months into quarantine in New Jersey, a state hard-hit by
Covid-19, I took my four-year-old daughter, who is biracial, to a
drive-thru ice cream parlor about twenty minutes from our home.
It was 3:30 pm, and I'd been teaching high school online since mid-
March. We just needed to get out of the house.

On our way, we passed by a large protest being held on Route
130 in Willingboro, the town where my mother grew up. They
held handmade signs, wore masks, and asked the cars to beep in

solidarity. The group cheered when I laid on my horn, perhaps encouraged that a white lady in a pickup truck agreed with them.

My daughter asked what all of the people were doing. I was driving and couldn't look back at her in the car seat behind me, but I told her that for a long time, people with white skin were terribly mean to people with darker skin like Daddy. I had introduced the concept of slavery a few days before when I told her that everything has a price and she replied, "Not people. You can't buy people." I had to tell her there was a time when other people did.

Our house had already been heavy with the deaths of Ahmaud Arbery and Breonna Taylor, so that when George Floyd was suffocated on Memorial Day, my husband, usually the bubbly life of the party, had retreated to his office during most of the waking hours. I asked my daughter if she'd recognized how sad her Daddy had been over the past few weeks. She said she had and I told her these people with the signs were sad, too. They were upset.

"What do their signs say?" she asked.

"They say that they matter, that they're beautiful, that they're worthy of love and justice and life. They say that they don't want people to hurt them anymore."

"That's good," she said plainly.

I asked, "What do you think about Daddy and Mommy not having the same color skin?"

I could see her shrug in the rearview mirror. "It's normal. You're a nice white person and you don't hurt people like Daddy."

I quietly wept until we reached the drive-thru window.

The last time my husband visited his mother, who still lives in Tulsa, he said she was headed to a protest in North Tulsa, where she and all of the descendants of the survivors of the Tulsa Race Massacre still live. When the white people killed Black people and burned down Black Wall Street in 1921, they also chased all of the

Black residents to the northern border of the city, which is where the terrorized and threatened community made their new home. They never got their old homes or businesses back.

My mother-in-law was protesting the opening of yet another Dollar General on the Northside, which was already inundated with dollar stores and unhealthy food options. There are no grocery stores of any kind on the Northside. You'll have to go South for that, where the white community of Tulsa continues to thrive to this day. On the Southside, you'll find the restaurants, hotels, movie theaters, bakeries, and all other places to spend your money. My husband's mother was organizing a boycott of the Dollar General, demanding that the Northside's status as a food desert come to an end.

That was almost two years ago. There is still no grocery store in North Tulsa.

The piano player at Greenwood Christian Center was named Joey Crutcher. He was always kind to me whenever he saw me at the church. He was a stocky Black man, broad-shouldered like my husband, and bald. When I was nineteen, I tried out for the praise team and Joey accompanied me on the keyboard for my audition. I ended up joining an independent choir, perhaps as the token white girl, and traveled the city with them instead, but all of the musicians in Tulsa, of which there are many, knew Joey and the Crutcher family.

When police gunned down Joey's younger brother Terrence in the summer of 2016, I did watch that video. The footage started automatically as I was scrolling through Facebook on my phone. The video was captured from the helicopter overhead and that angle let me have enough psychic distance from the event to view it. The pilot remarked that Terrence Crutcher looked like, "a bad dude," who "may be on something." The murderer, Betty Shelby, claimed that she thought he was going to his vehicle for a gun. No weapons were recovered from his car. It was around this time that I started praying every time my husband had to drive anywhere alone. I had been fearful in the past, understanding the inherent danger race played in my husband's life and the lives of other Black men like him, but Terrence's killing touched my personal life. My husband, in all his stocky glory, could be perceived as a "bad dude" to some officer one day, too.

I made the mistake of watching HBO's series, *Watchmen*, without much background information. I didn't think I was going into it blindly because I had watched the 2009 film of the same name long before. It opens with a young Black boy watching a silent film as his mother accompanies the movie on a piano. The empty theater was the first signal to me that something terrible was about to happen. I had no idea that once I left the velvet chairs of the movie house with the boy, Will Reeves, I would be hurled into the middle of the Tulsa Race Massacre happening just outside. Bodies dragged by wagons, people shot at point-blank range, successful businesses pillaged and burned. I gripped my shirt with my hands and sobbed for the rest of the episode. I told my husband that I was unprepared for the opening and asked him to watch the pilot episode on his own so that we could watch the rest of the series together and I wouldn't have to relive the nightmare that was his real-life ancestors' experience. What a privilege to be able to turn away.

On the way home from getting ice cream that day, my daughter and I took the same route that took us by the protest again. It was wrapping up and the police stopped traffic to allow the people to cross back over into Willingboro from the other side of the road. We were right at the light when this happened, so we had a lot of time to sit and watch the protesters with their signs walk past. My daughter and I talked some more about people with white skin hurting people with black and brown skin and why that's so wrong. Once traffic started moving again, she told me, "I'm so glad Daddy has his sword."

The blunt, couldn't-cut-through-steak ninja sword had followed us from that tiny apartment in Tulsa back to my native New Jersey six years ago. My husband still keeps it by his bedside, believing his brute strength could turn it into a real weapon. A pacifist by nature, even I wanted to be encouraged, like my daughter was, that it will be enough to keep him safe in America.

My Rabid Boy

by Dan Rosenberg

after Yehuda Amichai

My rabid boy: Each evening
he thrashes my fancy, catches
my every idea in his teeth.
He tears them. I am his woodland.
I feel him sharpen his claws
on my heart. I hear
his mews and snarls circle
each hair on my neck.

My rabid boy, my tarantula
stitching a nest of my hunger,
shushing my efforts at speech.
I crawl inside him.

I want to cock my ears
behind his ears,
like how under a cloud the owl
freezes, gathers herself,
and dives to transmute a vole.

Sugar on Snow

by Rosalie Davis

Everyone was home for the wake, even those who were tired from sitting with Papa Ned and waiting. He had made them wait so long. The floors in the house were pickled with sand and salt from people wearing boots inside. It was April, but spring was coming late. Snow lay heavy on the fields; during the day it melted and packed down, and at night it froze again. The light was coming back, though, and the snowshoe hares were changing color and were mottled, like they always were this time of year.

The morning had been gray, you could say pearly, but the clouds were thinning and it looked like the sun might yet show itself before dark. One of the younger boys wanted to go outdoors before supper. Sam said if Papa were still here, we wouldn't be sitting around indoors; we would all be out checking sap lines. But nobody had tapped the trees and there would be no sugaring off this year. Sam was looking out the window; he thought about the taste of sugar on snow, how it came from the trees and sky, but tasted of earth, parsnips, and the garden.

Finally Sadie, one of the older cousins, put on her coat and took him outdoors. They were just going to walk back to see if the ice was breaking up on the beaver pond below the fourth field. The fog was lifting in the pines, and the fine wet branches at the tops of the beeches looked like black veins against the hazy sky. Anybody watching from the living room could see the young people go out of sight, slipping under the second bar gate and dissolving into the woods.

Now it had been at least an hour since they went out of sight, and anybody watching could see Sam and Sadie coming back the way they had gone and stepping into the prints they had made going out. They were crossing the first field and were almost to the big boulder in the middle when they stopped. They were looking at the ground. The boy was counting springtails. The girl was noticing how the snow had changed and looked like frozen tears, the way it did after Nanna had poured the hot syrup over the fresh-packed pan of snow, and you were waiting.

The two stood up and started walking again. They were warm now and their coats were open. Sam's was worn at the cuffs and the waistband and suddenly looked too small for him. It had a patch on the chest with a gold lion and under the lion it said "Scotland The Brave." Papa had given it to him, and Nanna had sewed it on when the jacket was new. Now the patch was coming off and curling, and the lion's head and the words had disappeared and you could only see the lion's feet and the brush of its tail.

Sam and Sadie stopped again. Later they would tell that there was a sound coming off the field, like a long sigh or whisper in the woods they had just passed through. Like the whine the ice makes when it starts to break up on the pond, or the humming in an electrical circuit that is shorting out. But the pond was too far away to hear the ice break up, and the power line was a mile away.

"It must be the wind," Sadie said.

"But there isn't any wind," Sam said.

"I know," she said. "I've never heard it before."

"Me neither!" Sam said. Then he started to run back. As he ran, he had remembered how when Papa laid on the couch all winter, he had told him he wasn't afraid of anything anymore. In a soft voice, Papa had said that after he died he would become the fields, the trees, the rocks, the North Star, the sun, the clouds, the snow, the moonlight on the snow, the white hares in winter and the brown in summer, even the maple sugar. All the things he loved he would become. And when you are outdoors, his grandfather had told him, I would still be with you. That was when Papa knew he was only dreaming, the boy thought, before he was sure there was a real Abenaki camped behind the springhouse.

When Sam ran, Sadie had stood still, like when they played freeze tag at recess. Then she zipped up her jacket and walked to the big rock and leaned against it. She wanted to show Sam there was nothing to be afraid of. She wanted not to be afraid of anything. On top the rock was a big roll of barbed wire. Papa had wanted to get all of it out of the old-line fences, and the fields, and the woods, but he was always finding another line to pull. There wasn't enough time in the world to get it all out.

Barbwire was pure hell, he was always saying. Even if the wire was flat on the ground it could trip you and bring you face down. You might think you had been shot, it would happen that fast. Sadie could remember the time when Papa was cutting up an old maple and he had snagged a piece with the chain saw, and how the wire had lashed out and ripped his jacket and ruined the saw. She watched Sam run up the porch and go in the house.

To Sadie, each barb looked like a tiny pair of horns. She took off her mitten and touched one of the sharp cold points. She was sure now, surer than before, that sound had not been the ghost of anyone pulling wire, or anything like that. It wasn't so strange after all that Papa Ned had died, just that he had gone so slow.

Of course, an arrow might be swift, and whistle like that too. She thought now of the high stone ledge of the foundation in the cellar where Papa kept a beauty he had found ages ago, way back of the fourth field. Long and sharp it was, with the feathers still intact, too expensive to waste on small game or target practice. Only squirrels and crow were in season now, Sadie knew, and she didn't like to think a hunter trying to get away with something bigger had been so near, might still be near.

From out of her pocket, Sadie drew a small copper bell she carried wherever she went. Made for a heifer, it was not half so loud as the bull bell, but it was surprising how far its fine bright sound could travel. She was going to tell Uncle Warren; this was a story he would hear. And when at last the snow melted, and the ground thawed enough for Papa to be buried, and the trilliums bloomed, everyone could go together to post all the line fences, just as they did every year.

Stepping away from the big rock, Sadie began to ring the bell, slowly at first, just to signal she was still there and she was ok, just in case anyone was listening. As she got closer to the house, she could see Sam and Warren at the window, looking for her. She began to shake the bell harder, and then she started to run. As she ran she hoped that in the morning she would find the arrow.

What We Worried About

by L.M. Brown

Articles written by experts told us never to rush our children, but some mornings we couldn't help shouting at our children to *Come on, why are you so slow, you're driving me crazy.* When they were on the school bus, we worried they were little balls of tension because of us. We worried about getting their homework done at night. Computer screens lit up our children's faces and they startled if we came into the room.

"Are you doing your homework?"

"Yes."

We knew they weren't, and they'd just closed a screen they didn't want us to see because they were like cats with their back arched, but we couldn't call them liars. If we called them liars, wouldn't they become liars? Their sense of identity came from us, didn't it?

We lost sleep over the wrong things we said. The articles said we shouldn't say *Good job* or *Good Girl,* or *Well Done.* If we said *Good job* our children would need affirmation for everything they did.

They wouldn't be happy with their own successes. They would complete tasks only to make other people happy.

Our daughters would become the girls who did anything to please their man or woman, while losing themselves in the process. Our sons would too, though they would be more aggressive in their attention-seeking. We knew this because another article told us that *men* have a more extensively developed violence-related cognitive network *than women.*

We worried because, without realizing what we were doing, we'd put pressure on our children by telling them that *Practice makes perfect.* Unbeknown to ourselves, we would make them feel worthless. We told them that they weren't perfect because what they showed us was obviously not good enough. *Do not use the word perfect. Do not use the word perfect.* It became our nighttime chant before going to sleep, so we would remember tomorrow not to damage our children with such a word.

Do not use the word Okay — we said that the moment we woke up. It was the morning reflection, because the psychologist who studied children for decades wrote that if a child falls and is crying from sore knees, it is not okay to tell him that he is okay, because that is clearly not true. The child is hurt so you should say, *I know you're hurt,* and then you need to say something else.

We worried that we may fumble on this one, but habits need to be broken, especially ones that cause lasting damage, so we said, *I know you are hurt, and that was a scary fall.* And our children knew it was a scary fall, and they were crying for a reason and in this way, they learned how to deal with emotions.

We worried because we chipped at our children's independence. We didn't realize when our children were having difficulty with that puzzle we should have stayed in the background and asked questions about the pieces, *Do you think this piece would fit, is it too small, or too big?* Instead we jumped in and lent a helping hand and undermined their ability. We got too excited.

We clapped when we got a piece to fit and we thought in our moment of delight our children were happy too. We didn't think that we were too controlling until we read the articles. The next time our children asked us to do the puzzle with them, we said no. We said, *I'll just linger in the background and ask questions when you have a problem.*

Then that night when our children were asleep and the puzzle was on the floor, only half-done, and our children had cried from frustration, we worried that we didn't comfort them enough about their inability to finish the puzzle. When they cried, we nearly said, *it's okay*, but caught ourselves in time, only to make the dire mistake of telling them that there would be no dessert until they ate their dinner, thereby, lessening their value of the food and increasing their value of the treat.

We worried about telling our children that we couldn't afford their new bike or a holiday in Hawaii because we gave our children unnecessary worry and concern. We let them think that we were not in control of our finances. Our finances were wild horses getting away from us. We should have said, *No, we are not going to Hawaii, because we are saving our money for other things*, though it's possible that our children would think that their needs were not important. They were second best.

We worried about the grey roots starting to show, always on the top of our heads in sight of all and sundry. We worried about the creases on our skin that were visible when we studied our faces in the mirror, or the weight we'd put on and our need to go on a diet, and the importance of never saying that word in front of our children.

We worried that the kitchen needed a paint and our posts in Facebook weren't original enough, but mostly we worried about the day our children would start using Facebook.

We worried that the dinner wouldn't look the same as it did on the recipe book, though we knew that was impossible and nothing ever looked like the photos in recipe books. When our dinners tasted awful, we couldn't say *practice makes perfect*, because perfect was a bad word. We couldn't get annoyed when our children complained about cleaning up after dinner and remind them that we do everything for them, because then they would feel like a burden to us. They would think our duties were done out of responsibility, not love.

Those were the old fears.

We no longer worry about stressing our children by telling them to hurry up because time has stopped. We don't have to get our children ready for school or bite our tongues when they want to tie their laces or dress themselves because the days are wide open spaces. We look out the window at the desolate streets and drive by the closed stores, and we don't have to tell our children that we are saving up for something else, because there is nothing to save up with, and they've stopped asking about the new toy or the holiday in Hawaii. They are at the window too, seeing the emptiness, and they are hit with the silence that is brought with the absence of other children.

When our children come to us, we tell them we do not know what will happen. We tell them to take one day at a time. We worry about their grandparents going to the store, and their aunts and uncles working in the hospital. We no longer count down the days to summer holidays but count the people who have been lost. We give them names, we say he is a father, a brother, a son, she is a mother, a sister, a daughter. We listen to the teenager locked in her room crying because she misses her friends. We forget about the dishes in the sink.

We used to worry that our children didn't wash their hands, but it was a small worry, a worry that came after all the things we shouldn't say and how we were building them up into the adults they would become. We used to worry that they might get sick or fall or get hurt, but we didn't send their friends away in fear of them getting ill, or make sure they walked on the other side of the road far from people. We didn't hold them at night for long periods and think that if we got sick, they would get sick too. We didn't hold them tighter with the thought of them in hospital, their bodies like dolls under the sheet with no one beside them.

Outlander Blues

by Artress Bethany White

after quarantine binge-watching

I did not stay up to pen a poem
while screening Scottish history
slipshod neo-porn
with unaccented moans.
This series has got me going
five episodes a day
no end in sight
just me working to justify
lost hours of my life.
I'm not kidding myself, nor do I believe
these kilt-skirted men are kin to me.
They drink whiskey at every turn
betwixt and between wars
gory knife assaults and corded whip scars.
When Jamie says *Claire*, it gurgles like a curse
way back in his throat
as if he might end up
with spittle spraying from his mouth.
Then there's the ubiquitous red hair–
daughter Brianna more persimmon
than her pumpkin spice progenitor.
I hate these characters, my brain rails,
yet I've grown used to seeing
Jamie's tight arse and Claire's 34 Bs,
and the way they lunge at each other

as if they've never kissed before
at the end of every other scene.
Still, if I hear one more uttered
Bairn or *Kin ta ya*…
I don't know what I might do.
And no one, not one of them,
bathes enough for me.

Song at the End of the Mind
by Susan Rich

I think of you as a radio frequency—
sometimes hard to find

as I touch the illuminated dial.
But tonight you arrive

murmuring into my ear in halfsleep;

you offer a suitcase of small pleasures
and laughter that somersault across the country.

In this time of shelter in place,
we are fevered wanderers

with nothing but an open screen;

handheld devices offering luminous ellipses.
We heal the earthquaked bones

of our pasts decorating rough mouths
with new vocabularies—

no longer deferred.

As the world quiets,
I'm awake to our longings.

All that is left: to congregate
close along the shoreline

unbandaged and unadorned;

to listen to the smooth rhythm and blues
of Quarantine Radio.

This one goes out to you.

Crumbs

by Laura Bernstein-Machlay

I'm prone to guilt, coming as it does in crumbs and great big slices. Or sometimes as the entire pie. I feel it right now as Steven and Celia and I isolate from COVID-19 in our pretty house in Detroit—a city hit particularly hard by the virus.

In the midst of such loss, my little family and I are afforded the gifts of time and security by essential workers who, among other things, sell me absurdly cheap gas and prepare our prescriptions. The folks who process veggies and cereal and low-fat protein bars, who transport them, load shelves with them at Kroger's where I arrive sanitized, masked, and gloved to pick them up and whisk them safely home. Hence my current pie o'guilt.

As a writer and college teacher, I'm deemed utterly nonessential, as is my husband Steven, a chef-instructor. Our 19-year-old daughter Celia (always vital) returned home when her college classes went online, so she's stuck here, too, all of us snug as grubs in this house-bubble where food, specifically dinner, has become the lynchpin of our long days.

Food and I always had a complicated relationship. It's the mother that rocked me to sleep as a child. It's the lover I crave even as I deny myself its richer pleasures (the better to avoid guilt). I'm also a dull sort of cook who only passed junior high home economics by the grace of a teacher who ignored my bleeding chicken-a-la-king and flat, dense-as-a-brick soufflés. Meanwhile, there's Celia with her hundred food aversions, the textures she (ew!) eschews, components that can't (ever!) touch, and sauces (gasp!)—anathema.

"Hey," says Celia as she reads this over my shoulder, everyone being in each other's business right now.

"Hi, kid."

"I eat some sauces. Sometimes. I've gotten adventurous since going to college."

"Good to know."

Her expanded palate will certainly be a gift to my dear, beleaguered Steven—because what's a poor chef to do, stuck home with two women who refuse to enjoy the breadth of his culinary gifts. Steven, who believes pie is a necessary food group and butter a minor god. That every texture matters. That calories are a mispronounced city in Alberta, Canada—in other words, entirely off topic.

"Do you mean Calgary?" asks Steven as he reads this over my shoulder.

"You got it."

"Huh," he says, and wanders away.

Steven's generally good-natured, as are we all, but due to my family's different food sensibilities, dinnertime has always been problematic for us. Either the cook-of-the-night (usually me for whatever reason) prepared multiple meals, or everybody grazed. In other words, we displayed good ol' American individualism and fended for ourselves. Which, unsurprisingly, raised in me a whole crop of guilt, even as I threw up my hands and gave in to it.

But now everything's changed. We're sheltering together 24/7. The daily news explodes like bullets. The street outside our windows has gone silent and empty as a new planet.

During the day, Steven and I might retreat to separate rooms as we navigate online courses, and Rip Van Celia—nearly nocturnal at this point—barely drags herself awake for her own classes before nodding off again. But at least family dinner is communal now, and it's taken on new urgency. Created as it is from elements gathered and driven, stocked and sold by strangers risking their lives for our comfort, how could it be otherwise?

It boils down to this: some evenings I give in and bliss-out on Steven's carb and butter-laden masterpieces, or Celia attempts a bite or two of something squishy (ew!). Other nights, we graze, but we do it in the same room, and our dinner might consist of Cheerios, cottage cheese and parsley that's risen like hope in our garden, on pickles and Nutella toast (gasp! not at the same time), on s'mores toasted in the fireplace, on radishes and Flamin' Hot Cheeto's. Or, ya know, a low-fat protein bar and yogurt for me.

Which is fine. For this moment (don't blink, or you'll miss it!) we're together. It's a gift we didn't notice enough pre-virus. One which, for the space of dinnertime, transforms guilt to gratitude. Just a little bit—because how could it be otherwise in this breaking world? Still, I gather the crumbs in my hands. I swallow them whole.

Love in the Time of COVID-19: Have Our Lives Changed Forever? I Sure Hope.
by J.R. Jamison

Our little mid-century ranch, with its limestone exterior and big picture window, sits clustered together with other mid-century homes—tri-levels and A-frames—in a neighborhood that straddles the bustling city limits and acres of farmland that stretch out across rural Delaware County, Indiana. This proximity to civilization, yet freedom to get lost on a back road, is what drew my husband, Cory, and me to the house when we bought it in 2005. When our realtor walked us through we whispered into each other's ears about backyard picnics and late-night escapades with glasses of wine. The real selling point, though, was that big picture window in the front room and the way it scattered morning sunlight across the pine-wood floors.

A few months after moving into our new house, I took a job an hour-and-a-half away, which meant I had to get up at 4:30 every morning to make the commute. I didn't return until 6:30 each evening. It wasn't long until Cory decided to explore his passion—medicine—and went back to school. As each year passed, we celebrated milestones in our life: Cory's graduation and job placement in an ER the next town over; my founding of a storytelling nonprofit and its show on NPR. Our life was late nights in hospitals and studios and grabbing dinner on the go. We had promotions, and speaking engagements, and work travel, and even more travel on top of that. While our life felt exciting, we saw less and less of each other; and those backyard picnics became something of a distant memory. Our mid-century with its big picture window and sunlit wood floors had become only a place where we slept and showered.

The nights Cory and I found ourselves home together we sat at opposite ends of the couch and scrolled through social media, interacting with the devices in our hands but not with each other. Post after post, meme after meme, all seemingly about why a Democrat shouldn't be trusted or why a Republican should be hated. Threads of arguments and infighting within Parties between moderates and progressives; but no common ground. Facebook and Twitter had become cesspools of the divides in our country, and yet we couldn't stop watching as tiring and stressful as it had become. This was downtime in our house.

As January 2020 approached, we had our calendars filled through September, and I cringed anytime someone reached out about getting together. Trying to find the time to fit one more thing into our already busy schedules seemed offensive. I often found myself frustrated with friends and family and thinking: *Why can't people be better planners?*

And then COVID-19 happened.

Like the rest of the U.S. we saw images on the news from China, and read stories of despair as it crept into other parts of Asia; but somehow we thought we were immune. We went on with life as if a pandemic couldn't happen to us. In late February I spoke with a group in Tennessee about an upcoming appearance, and there was no talk of the virus or even the possibility of postponing or canceling. Then we finally woke up. *Was it the videos from Italy begging us to take this seriously? Was it the surge in New York?*

I still don't know when we recognized this was real, other than one by one in the days that followed I erased our lives from the calendar. The speaking engagement in Seattle, gone. The trip to Cyprus, bye-bye. My niece's bridal shower, *auf wiedersehen*. The research travel for my book, kaput. We suddenly had nothing through July.

At first I was depressed. I threw the covers over my head and cried. I gripped our sheets between my fists and screamed. Then guilt set in because people were losing their businesses, others were dying, and we were healthy. The virus hadn't touched anyone we knew and we both still had our jobs.

I pulled the covers from my head. "Am I being selfish?"

Cory rubbed my back to console me. "It's okay to be sad about your losses, sweet pea."

I spent the rest of the night at the intersection of grief and gratitude.

The next evening we began to binge everything we could find on Netflix and Hulu. We're now on week seven of isolation. Between episodes of *Ozark* we take breaks and check our phones. I scroll and see posts from old friends—those whose feeds were once on opposite ends of the political spectrum than my own—who now binge the same show. I leave comments about predictions but ask for no spoilers. Cory and I settle back into the couch, our feet finding their way toward each other under the blanket, and we click the remote to begin the next episode. After a few, we turn off the TV and stay up late talking.

In the mornings I sip my coffee in the front room and watch the sun trace shadows across the pine-wood floor until the entire space becomes a theatre of light, and then I check email for a bit. In the afternoons we walk our dog around the neighborhood, and yell out across the street at our neighbor who's enjoying the smells of spring from the safety of her opened garage. We've finally taken drives on those back roads.

Life has slowed and I wonder what of our newfound habits will remain. We'll get back to our commutes, our speaking engagements, our travel. This won't last forever; yet I'm already beginning to mourn the loss of this way of living. I hope future me says no more often to needless opportunities that fill our calendar; that I still call my mom and dad each day to talk about movies and the grocery store; and that Cory and I still tangle our feet together in the evenings as we binge another show.

Yesterday we cooked dinner and made a picnic in our backyard. Cory shook a fleece blanket in the air and let it drift to the ground; I placed the food in the middle. We sat together, no one else in sight other than a few robins singing in our budding oak. After we ate we held hands and took in the sounds of our neighborhood: mowers buzzing in the distance; barking dogs; kids laughing. I opened my notebook to scribble a few words about the moment and saw something I had written last fall after visiting the Mediterranean:

Though we may try to turn the tides of time in one direction or another, we must live in the now and learn from its lessons.

I looked around at our fenced-in yard, our little mid-century ranch with its limestone exterior, at my husband. This life is enough.

Time & Motion Studies: Diagnostic

by Judson Evans

I tied a naked guy up to a bedpost once. I had to go over
his instructions carefully before setting out, the door was
unlocked, room left dark, just enough bread crumbs.

Time seems to slow down at night.
If it was not for cold and snow, I would not
realize that it is winter. Time seems to stop
altogether.

The history of cinema is cognate to the history
of trains. What they call sprouts in the photograph
are objects reaching out of
frame, lured by the light.

I do not know my age.
My age does not seem to change.
I cannot imagine myself older than I am.

I remember how they leapt
for the bell rope in the church, how the weight
of the bell lofted them. I don't remember
who they were or what they were married to.
Treat it as a double thickness, the lashing together of then
and now.

There are languages in which the future is behind,
the past ahead.
I hardly pay attention to the sequence of day and night.
They teach their children to walk backward
toward tombs of the ancestors.

Anything can be turned into a pinhole camera,
even this house if we covered every window and door,
just one well-timed pinprick– the long exposure.

Shame and Blessings at the Coin-Op
by Joelle Fraser

Just before the virus drifted into the world, a friend I'd recently met texted that she was nervous. Her washing machine had broken at the worst time, just before a trip.

I have to go to the laundromat! she wrote; I could picture the shudder as she added the scream emoji. I understood. Laundromats can be dingy, sometimes dangerous, places. Even the nicer ones offer little appeal. For many people, going to a storefront to wash your clothes is like going to the thrift store to buy kitchenware.

My friend was also unsure of etiquette. In a place of such weird intimacy, do you avert your eyes from someone's laid out socks and pajamas? She didn't want people knowing the color of her sheets and towels. In some ways, doing your laundry at home was social distancing before it ever became a thing.

Her candor told me she wasn't aware that I don't have a washer or dryer myself. Not since my divorce ten years ago, in fact, have I had the convenience of doing a wash right in my home—of doing a light load just because I wanted to wear a certain outfit, or because my son spilled juice on his favorite blanket. But my home is so small, and the expense never seemed justified.

When people do find out, they react with surprise, then veiled pity. Lacking these appliances seems just steps away from home-lessness. The washer/dryer is a tangible symbol, like the bike a man rides in tattered coat because he doesn't have a car. To haul your dirty clothes, your rumpled used bedding, through the parking lot is to admit you're a have-not.

When the stay-at-home orders hit the news and our lives, I was worried not just about food and hoarders and falling enrollment in my writing classes. As a single mom of a teenage boy, I need to wash clothes once a week—at least. So while my Facebook friends were figuring out how to get food delivered, I was researching where to wash our clothes.

It turns out that even during a quarantine, laundromats are "essential," at least for some people. So even though it's a risk, I can still go to Mr. Bubbles, a mile from my house, next to a tiny *car-niceria* where Latino construction workers eat lunch while watching Spanish soccer on the mounted TV, and where I often order a burrito to-go. The other establishment is Woodrow's Tavern, whose drifting cigarette smoke I can smell forty feet away. Of course it's closed now.

At Mr. Bubbles, most of the patrons during the pandemic are still female, towing small kids and bundles of colorful clothes. I'm the rare white woman, though plenty of old white men frequent the place. Some are truckers, stopping off on the road; others are just alone. Sometimes there's a couple, and their easy rhythm of folding together reveals they've done this for years, if not decades.

I do see people who are homeless sometimes, but more often it's simply people who live lives of scarcity. They come in battered cars and pick-up trucks and campers that could use a wash, too.

Even the laundromat has its class distinctions—you can tell by the laundry sacks and baskets, if they're new and matching, or if the loads are dragged in, heaped and bulging, in dusty and torn garbage bags.

There's a different tension now when I go. People are wary, keeping the distance we've been instructed to observe. I watch the women with their children and remember my own single mother standing in front of a pile of tangled clothes while I ran around with the other kids; we'd beg for snacks from the vending machine, for the arcade game that usually was broken, swallowing precious money. These mothers and I exchange amused glances, a sigh and a shrug as a child dashes past, buzzed out and bored.

I can't help but wonder how many of these people have lost their jobs. We're a hospitality state here in Nevada, after all. And how many won't get stimulus checks for whatever reason—a choked system, fear of the government? Where does that old couple go after their clothes are done? It may be that they live in that camper in the parking lot, the one with the little yapping dog.

The last time I did my laundry, people were more quiet than usual, and so the sound of hardship seemed louder: *plinka clinka clink*. Sixteen times for a $4 wash. Eight minutes of drying time for a quarter (never enough). With some people, you can almost see the pain it costs, coin by vanishing coin.

"We're all in this together, you know," I told my son the other day. "Rich and poor." He will remember it all—how when he was little he liked to exchange the five-dollar bill for the quarters, to push those coins into the machines. In middle school he helped me haul in our baskets. These are the kinds of lessons that are breathed in, that can't be learned through movies and books, or by a drive over to the poor side of the tracks, to see how others live. We often leave his outgrown clothes in a pile, with a note "free" taped on top, and sometimes, before our last load is dry, the offering is gone.

Maybe people suppose I feel deprivation because I have to leave the house to wash our clothes—and that the poverty it suggests taints me. And it's true, during this time of uncertainty, I do sometimes wish I could stay safely inside and listen to the comforting hum of the dryer in the other room. Ultimately, though, I feel the opposite: going to the laundromat makes me see how much we do have. And that helps, now that the edge feels closer.

Now and then, as I drive home to my warm, humble home, gratitude fills me with such swift force I can't breathe. How lucky, I tell myself and my son: how lucky we are to be alive.

How Lonely Sat the Town

by Julia Story

Quarry houses like napping men flanked us. We were born
on the day of other births, many other births.

Inside the train tracks were the sounds of sleep, and within
the miniature of a single word was our story. You were

my widow, you paced many nights while I slept
and placed in me the sad horses of night. Grass creaked

as it grew. Summer afternoons were many miles long,
and we twisted in and out of each other like other humans moving

in and out of their lungs or their shame. Some days we woke up
already dead. Then the birds lifted our prone bodies and carried us

above the gray houses, the empty crumbs of people, a mute strip mall
too stricken to look up to see us. When the birds tired

still we floated, the space in us having learned to become its own sky,
our own gravities shattered, our bodies filled with approaching

dawns. When we died for good, we went back into our separate seas,
and the spaces we had spent our lives opening

became another town so far away we never made it there.

Contributors

Jonathan B. Aibel is a poet who spends his days wrestling software to the ground as an engineer specializing in quality and testing. His poems have been published, or will soon appear, in *Rogue Agent*, *Main Street Rag*, *Constellations*, *Nixes Mate*, *Lily Poetry Review*, and elsewhere. He has studied with Lucie Brock-Broido, David Ferry and Barbara Helfgott Hyett. Jonathan lives in Concord, MA, with his family.

Rachel Abramowitz's poems and reviews have appeared in *American Poetry Review*, *Tin House Online*, *The Threepenny Review*, *Seneca Review*, *The Kenyon Review Online*, *Crazyhorse*, *Tupelo Quarterly*, and others. She is a graduate of the Iowa Writers' Workshop and the University of Oxford, and has taught English Literature at Barnard College in New York.

Tracey Anderson is currently a public school Instructional Technology Specialist at Provincetown IB Schools on Cape Cod in Massachusetts. She graduated from Edinburgh College of Art in Scotland, where she studied Drawing and Painting. She draws every day. Her work can be seen and supported at: www.poorhooligans.com

José Angel Araguz is a CantoMundo fellow and the author of seven chapbooks as well as the collections *Everything We Think We Hear*, *Small Fires*, *Until We Are Level Again*, and, most recently, *An Empty Pot's Darkness*. His poems, creative nonfiction, and reviews have appeared in *Crab Creek Review*, *Prairie Schooner*, *New South*, *Poetry International*, and *The Bind*. Born and raised in Corpus Christi, Texas, he runs the poetry blog *The Friday Influence* and composes erasure poems on the Instagram account @poetryamano. A faculty member in Pine Manor College's Solstice Low-Residency MFA program, he also reads for the journal *Right Hand Pointing*. With an MFA from New York University and a PhD from the University of Cincinnati, José is an Assistant Professor of English at Suffolk University in Boston where he also serves as Editor-in-Chief of *Salamander Magazine*.
Twitter: https://twitter.com/josearaguz
Instagram: https://www.instagram.com/poetryamano/
Personal site: https://thefridayinfluence.wordpress.com/

Khem K. Aryal's fiction has appeared in such journals as *Isthmus, Hawai'i Pacific Review, Poydras Review, Northeast Review, Warscapes,* and *Qwerty Magazine*. He teaches creative writing at Arkansas State University, Jonesboro, and also serves as Creative Materials Editor of *Arkansas Review*.

Charles Bernstein is the author of *Near/Miss* and *Pitch of Poetry*. ROOF recently published *The Course*, a collaboration with Ted Greenwald. The poems in this issue are forthcoming in the author's collection, *Topsy Turvy*, from the University of Chicago Press, Spring, 2021. He lives in Brooklyn.

Laura Bernstein-Malachy's writing has appeared in many magazines including *The American Scholar, The Coachella Review, Georgia Review, Hotel Amerika, Into the Void, Michigan Quarterly Review* and others. She has essays forthcoming in the *Massachusetts Review* and *Gargoyle*. Her full-length collection of creative nonfiction essays, *Travelers*, was published in 2018. Find her at https://www.facebook.com/Laura-Bernstein-Machlay-830773183791593/ and http://laurabernsteinmachlayauthor.com.

L.M. Brown is the author of the novel *Debris* and collections *Were We Awake* and *Treading the Uneven Road*. Her stories have been nominated for the Pushcart prize and published in over a dozen literary magazines, such as *The Chiron Review, Eclectica, Litro, Fiction Southeast, Toasted Cheese* and more. Her novel *Hinterland* was published in 2020.

Lindsey Byars is the Communications Liaison for Concord University in Athens, West Virginia, a career she began after teaching high school English and theater for 11 years. She is pursuing her Master's in Creative Writing and Literature through Harvard University's Extension School. Lindsey published her first piece of writing in 2018, a feature article for *West Virginia South*, and she was a finalist in Shepherd University's 2018 West Virginia Fiction competition. Since then, she has contributed articles to *West Virginia Executive Magazine* and is a staff writer for Concord University publications.

Celeste Cosme is an MFA candidate at Rosemont College. She has taught high school English for fourteen years. Currently, she is working on a YA novel about kids at an alternative school in New Jersey, like the one she's at now. She lives with her photographer husband and curious four-year-old daughter. "For Greenwood" is her first published piece.

Rosalie Davis, a longtime Boston freelancer, has taught writing to adults in Cambridge and Brookline since 2012. Also set in the North Country, her essay "Tourniquet" appeared in *Pangyrus* Four. She has also contributed to *Green Mountains Review, UNH Magazine, UU World, Yankee Publications, Gardens Illustrated, The Wall Street Journal*, and *Horticulture Magazine*.

Wendy Drexler's third poetry collection, *Before There Was Before*, was published by Iris Press in 2017. Her poems have appeared or are forthcoming in *The Atlanta Review, Barrow Street, J Journal, Nimrod, Prairie Schooner, Salamander, The Mid-American Review, The Hudson Review, The Threepenny Review, The Worcester Review*, and the *Valparaiso Poetry Review*, among others; featured on *Verse Daily* and WBUR's *Cognoscenti*; and in numerous anthologies. She is the poet in residence at New Mission High School in Hyde Park, MA, and programming co-chair for the New England Poetry Club.

Martín Espada was born in Brooklyn, New York in 1957. He has published more than twenty books as a poet, editor, essayist and translator. His most recent book of poems from Norton is called *Floaters*. "The Stoplight at the Corner Where Somebody Had to Die" is from that collection. Other books of poems include *Vivas to Those Who Have Failed* (2016), *The Trouble Ball* (2011), *The Republic of Poetry* (2006), *Alabanza* (2003), *A Mayan Astronomer in Hell's Kitchen* (2000), *Imagine the Angels of Bread* (1996), *City of Coughing and Dead Radiators* (1993) and *Rebellion is the Circle of a Lover's Hands* (1990). He is the editor of *What Saves Us: Poems of Empathy and Outrage in the Age of Trump* (2019). His many honors include the Ruth Lilly Poetry Prize, the Shelley Memorial Award, the Robert Creeley Award, the National Hispanic Cultural Center Literary Award, an American Book Award, an Academy of American Poets Fellowship, the PEN/Revson Fellowship and a Guggenheim Fellowship. *The Republic of Poetry* was a finalist for the Pulitzer Prize. His book of essays and poems, *Zapata's Disciple* (1998), was banned in Tucson as part of the Mexican-American Studies Program outlawed by the state of Arizona, and reissued by Northwestern University Press. A former tenant lawyer, Espada is a professor of English at the University of Massachusetts-Amherst.

Judson Evans is a poet and visual artist, who has written and published in a variety of poetic forms and genres. He was Director of Liberal Arts at The Boston Conservatory for twenty-five years, and is now a full-time Professor of Liberal Arts at Berklee College of Music, where he teaches Literature, Poetry Workshops, and an elective humanities course on Paleolithic Cave Art. He has been a life-long enthusiast for all Japanese-based poetic forms and regularly publishes haiku, renku, and haibun in the main journals of those forms. He has been involved in a wide range of collaborative experiments with composers, choreographers, other poets, and most recently with videographer Ray Klimek. Evans has had his poems set to music by composers, such as Mohammed Farouz and Marti Epstein, and developed into dance pieces with choreographer/performance artist Julie Ince Thompson and the poetry dance collective teXtmoVes with Karen Klein. He was chosen as an "Emerging Poet" by John Yau for The Academy of American Poets in 2007, and won the Philip Booth Poetry Prize from Salt Hill Review in 2013. His poems have appeared most recently in *Folio*, *Volt*, *1913: a journal of forms*, and *Cutbank*.

Adam Fell is the author of two books of poetry: *Dear Corporation*, (Forklift Books 2019) and *I Am Not A Pioneer*. He has had more than thirty poems published in various journals and magazines, including *Tin House*; *Crazyhorse*; *Forklift, Ohio*; *Diagram*; *Sixth Finch*; *jubilat*; *Ocean State Review*; *Poets. org*; *Pinwheel*; *Matter*; and others. He is an Assistant Professor of English at Edgewood College in Madison, WI, where he co-curates the Monsters of Poetry reading series.

Joelle Fraser has published two memoirs (*The Territory of Men*, 2002, Random House; and *The Forest House*, 2013, Counterpoint Press). Her essays have appeared in journals including *Brevity*, *Crazyhorse*, *The Iowa Review*, *Michigan Quarterly Review*, *Fourth Genre*, and more. She teaches online at Creative Nonfiction. She lives in Reno, Nevada with her son and five rescue pets, where she's working on her third book.

Ryane Nicole Granados is a Los Angeles native and she earned her MFA in Creative Writing from Antioch University, Los Angeles. Her work has been featured in various publications including *Pangyrus*, *The Manifest-Station*, *Forth Magazine*, *The Nervous Breakdown*, *The Atticus Review* and *LA Parent Magazine*. Ryane is best described as a writer, professor and devoted wife and mom who laughs loud and hard, even in the most challenging of circumstances. Her storytelling has been nominated for a Pushcart Prize and showcased in the national stage production *Expressing Motherhood* and KP-CC's live series *Unheard LA*.

Michelle Gurule is a queer writer from Denver, Colorado. She is a second year MFA candidate in creative writing at the University of New Mexico, where she was *Blue Mesa Review*'s 2019-2020 nonfiction editor. Her nonfiction has been published in *Alien* and *Stirring*. Michelle is currently working on a memoir that explores sex work.

Karen Harris, Ed.D., is a teacher, writer, musician, and researcher. She taught at Brookline High School's democratic School within a School, and at the Favorite Poem Project. Her writing and research interests include parenting, education, friendship, poetry, ADHD, and rock and roll. She fronted the Boston rock band, The Vivs, and lives in Cambridge with her husband and kids. www.karenharris.org.

J.R. Jamison is a writer based in Indiana where he co-hosts The Facing Project Radio Show on NPR. His work has been featured in multiple journal outlets, including *The Guardian* and *The Huffington Post*. His debut memoir, *Hillbilly Queer*, is forthcoming (May 11, 2021). He is a two-time graduate of Ball State University with a Master of Arts in Education and a Bachelor of Science in Cultural Geography and Creative Writing. He can be found on Twitter @JR_Jamison.

Belle (Bom) Kim is a cartoonist and PhD candidate in English literature at University of Washington. Originally from Suwon, South Korea, she lives in Seattle with her husband and pet bunny. Her work has appeared or is forthcoming in Decomp Journal, The Normal School, and *Exposition Review*, and can be found at bunboti.com.

Xiaoly Li is a poet, photographer and computer engineer who lives in Massachusetts. Prior to writing poetry, she published stories in a selection of Chinese newspapers. Her photography, which has been shown and sold in galleries in Boston, often accompanies her poems. Her poetry is forthcoming or has recently appeared in *PANK, Atlanta Review, Chautauqua, Rhino, Whale Road Review, Rockvale Review, Cold Mountain Review, J Journal* and elsewhere. She has been nominated for Best of the Net, Best New Poets, and a Pushcart Prize. Xiaoly received her Ph.D. in electrical engineering from Worcester Polytechnic Institute and Masters in computer science and engineering from Tsinghua University in China.

Olive Malcolm, known to her friends as Polly, grew up in Illinois, then married and raised her four children in Massachusetts. For the last 36 years she has lived in Cambridge, MA.

Vi Khi Nao is the author of four poetry collections: *Human Tetris* (11:11 Press, 2019), *Sheep Machine* (Black Sun Lit, 2018), *Umbilical Hospital* (Press

1913, 2017), *The Old Philosopher* (winner of the Nightboat Prize for 2014). She is also the author of the short story collection, *A Brief Alphabet of Torture* (winner of the 2016 FC2's Ronald Sukenick Innovative Fiction Prize), and the novel, *Fish in Exile* (Coffee House Press, 2016). Her work includes poetry, fiction, film and cross-genre collaboration. She was the Fall 2019 fellow at the Black Mountain Institute. vikhinao.com

Pamela Painter is the author of four story collections: *Getting to Know the Weather, The Long and Short of It, Wouldn't You Like to Know,* and *Ways to Spend the Night.* Her stories have appeared in *The Atlantic, Five Points, Kenyon Review, SmokeLong Quarterly,* and *Ploughshares,* and in numerous anthologies such as *Sudden Fiction* and *Flash Fiction.* Her new collection *Fabrications: New and Selected Stories* was published by Johns Hopkins University Press in November 2020. Painter is one of five founding donors of the Flash Fiction Collection recently established at the Harry Ransom Center, University of Texas at Austin. She lives in Boston and teaches in the Emerson College MFA Program.

Pamela Petro is a writer, artist, and educator living in Northampton, MA. She's the author of three books of literary nonfiction, an artist's book, and a graphic script, and has widely exhibited her photography. She teaches creative writing on Lesley University's MFA Program and at Smith College, and is Co-Director of the Dylan Thomas Summer School in Creative Writing at the University of Wales, Trinity St David, where she is also a Fellow. She was educated at Brown University and the University of Wales. Pamela's forthcoming book is *The Long Field Field: A Memoir, Wales, and the Presence of Absence.* https://www.pamelapetro.com

Daniel E. Pritchard is a writer, translator, and founding editor of *The Critical Flame,* a journal of criticism and literary nonfiction. His work has been published by the *Kenyon Review Online, EuropeNow, SpoKe,* the *Los Angeles Review of Books, Harvard Review,* and *Missouri Review,* among others. He lives in Greater Boston.

Susan Rich, Seattle poet, is the author of four books of poetry, most recently, *Cloud Pharmacy* (Shortlisted for the Julie Suk Prize) and *The Alchemist's Kitchen* (Finalist for the Washington State Book Award). She has been granted a Fulbright Fellowship, the PEN USA Award for Poetry, the Times (of London) Literary Supplement Award and a 4Culture Grant. Rich's poems appear in *Harvard Review, New England Review, Poetry Ireland,* and *World Literature Today* among many other publications. She has two collections forthcoming: *A Gallery of Postcards and Maps: New and Selected Poems* (Salmon Press) and *Blue Atlas* (Red Hen Press).

Dan Rosenberg is the author of *cadabra* and *The Crushing Organ*, which won the American Poetry Journal Book Prize. He has also written two chapbooks, *A Thread of Hands* and *Thigh's Hollow*, which won the Omnidawn Poetry Chapbook Contest, and he co-translated Miklavž Komelj's *Hippodrome*. Rosenberg's poems have appeared recently in *Ploughshares*, *Conjunctions*, *North American Review*, and *Brooklyn Review*. He teaches literature and creative writing at Wells College in Aurora, NY.

Michael Salcman, poet, physician and art historian, was chairman of neurosurgery at the University of Maryland and president of the Contemporary Museum in Baltimore. His poems appear in *Alaska Quarterly Review*, *Arts & Letters*, *Hopkins Review*, *The Hudson Review* among others. Books include *The Clock Made of Confetti* (Orchises, 2007), nominated for The Poets' Prize, *The Enemy of Good is Better* (Orchises, 2011), *Poetry in Medicine*, his popular anthology of classic and contemporary poems on doctors, patients, illness & healing (Persea Books, 2015) and *A Prague Spring, Before & After* (2016), winner of the 2015 Sinclair Poetry Prize from Evening Street Press. *Shades & Graces*, his new collection from Spuyten Duyvil (2020), is the inaugural winner of The Daniel Hoffman Legacy Book Prize.

Judy Sandler is pursuing her Master's Degree in creative nonfiction from The University of Southern Maine's Stonecoast MFA program. Before graduate school, she taught English and elementary education in independent schools. She holds a Master's Degree in liberal arts from Johns Hopkins University. She has been published in *Edutopia*, an on-line educational journal, and *Collection Magazine*, the yearly publication of Friends School of Baltimore. She lives in Baltimore with her husband, with whom she has raised three grown children.

Jon Shorr has been a freelance writer for the Discovery Channel and for various magazines, including *JMore*, *Tricycle*, *Today's Education*, *Social Education*, and *Media & Methods*. His fiction and personal essays have been published in local and national journals and anthologies, including *Passager*, *The Inquisitive Eater*, *Defenestration*, *Stories That Need to Be Told*, *Psychopoetica*, and *Bluntly*. He is a University of Baltimore professor emeritus.

James Stewart III is a Black writer from Chicago. He has earned an MFA from the School of the Art Institute of Chicago and an MA from North

Central College. Stewart co-curates the Chicago-based reading series "The Guild Complex presents Exhibit B" and is managing editor of *Critics' Union Magazine*. His writing has appeared or is forthcoming in *580 Split, The Forge, Cleaver Magazine, Another Chicago Magazine*, and *Cowboy Jamboree*. This story is from his unpublished manuscript, "Defiant Acts," a novel about a multi-racial working-class family's daily struggles and the costs they pay for loving each other. www.jamesstewart3.com

Julia Story is the author of *Post Moxie* (Sarabande Books), winner of the 2009 Katherine A. Morton Prize and the *Ploughshares'* John C. Zacharis First Book Award; *The Trapdoor* (Dancing Girl Press); *Julie the Astonishing* (Sixth Finch Books); and *Spinster for Hire* (The Word Works). Her work has been awarded a Pushcart Prize and has appeared in many publications including *Diode, Ploughshares, The Paris Review, Sixth Finch*, and *The New Yorker*. She is from Indiana and now lives in Massachusetts.

Cole Swensen has published 17 volumes of poetry and a collection of critical essays, *Noise That Stays Noise*. A collection of hybrid poem-essays, *Art in Time*, from which this piece is taken, will be coming out from Nightboat Books in 2021. Most of her work is related to the visual arts and often addresses landscape and land-use concerns. A former Guggenheim fellow, she has been a finalist twice for the *LA Times* Book Award and once for the National Book Award and has been awarded the Iowa Poetry Prize, the SF State Poetry Center Book Award, and the National Poetry Series. She also translates poetry, prose, and art criticism from French and won the 2004 PEN USA Award in Literary Translation. She divides her time between Paris and Providence RI, where she teaches at Brown University.

Angelique Tung lives with her family in Wellesley, MA. Dedicated to supporting others who have experienced trauma, she is currently teaching writing workshops for 9/11 survivors through Voices of Resilience. She has spent the last ten years working in development and fundraising and has recently decided to pursue her MSW to continue her work with trauma survivors. "Mourning in the Time of COVID-19," is her first publication.

Susan Volchok, a New York writer, is a frequent contributor to *Pangyrus* and has published widely in journals and anthologies ranging from the *Virginia Quarterly Review* and the *Kenyon Review* to *Best American Erotica*, in mainstream magazines and newspapers including the *New York Times*, and online at *n+1, The Common, The Literary Bohemian*, and *Mr. Beller's Neighborhood*, among other sites. She has spent the better part of life on the Upper West Side of Manhattan, perfectly situated between Central Park and Riverside Park on the Hudson.

Artress Bethany White is Nonfiction Editor at *Pangyrus* and the author of the poetry collection *My Afmerica* (Trio House Press, 2019), and the essay collection *Survivor's Guilt: Essays on Race and American Identity* (New Rivers Press, 2020). Her prose and poetry have appeared in such journals as *Harvard Review, Tupelo Quarterly, The Hopkins Review, Pleiades, Solstice, Poet Lore, Ecotone,* and *Birmingham Poetry Review*. White has received the Mary Hambidge Distinguished Fellowship from the Hambidge Center for Creative Arts for her nonfiction, The Mona Van Duyn Scholarship in Poetry from the Sewanee Writers' Conference, and writing residencies at The Writer's Hotel and the Tupelo Press/MASS MoCA studios. She is associate professor of English at East Stroudsburg University in Pennsylvania and teaches poetry and nonfiction workshops for the Rosemont College Summer Writers Retreat.

Naomi J. Williams is the author of the novel *Landfalls* (FSG, 2015). Her short fiction and essays have appeared in many places, including *One Story, A Public Space, Electric Literature, Lit Hub,* and *Zoetrope,* garnering one Pushcart Prize, four Pushcart nominations, and a Best American honorable mention. The recipient of awards and fellowships from Hedgebrook, Djerassi, Willapa Bay, and the Sustainable Arts Foundation, she makes her home in Sacramento and teaches for the low-res MFA program at Ashland University.

About Pangyrus

Pangyrus is a Boston-based group of writers, editors, and creative professionals with a new vision for how high-quality writing can thrive on the internet. Now also a print publication, we aim to foster a community of creative individuals and organizations dedicated to art, ideas, and making culture thrive.

Combining Pangaea and gyrus, the terms for the world continent and whorls of the cerebral cortex crucial to verbal association, Pangyrus is about connection.

INDEX by AUTHOR